Women in Transition

Voices from Lithuania

Suzanne LaFont
Editor

State University of New York Press

Published by
State University of New York Press, Albany

© 1998 State University of New York

The essay *Marija Gimbutas: Tribute to a Lithuanian Legend*
by Joan Marler © 1996 by Joan Marler

For information, address State University of New York Press,
State University Plaza, Albany, N.Y. 12246

Production by E. Moore
Marketing by Anne M. Valentine

Library of Congress Cataloging-in-Publication Data

Women in transition : voices from Lithuania / [edited by] Suzanne
LaFont.
    p.   cm.
Includes bibliographical references and index.
ISBN 0-7914-3811-2 (hc : alk. paper). — ISBN 0-7914-3812-0 (pbk.
: alk. paper)
    1. Women—Lithuania. 2. Women—Lithuania—Social conditions.
3. Women—Lithuania—Economic conditions. I. LaFont, Suzanne,
1954–   .
HQ1665.9.W66   1998
305.42′094793—dc21   97-28022
                                                              CIP

10 9 8 7 6 5 4 3 2 1

Women
in
Transition

*This book is dedicated to
the Women of Lithuania
and
Eric LaFont Kaplan*

Contents

Editor's Preface

In the summer of 1994, when the Civic Education Project offered me a position teaching at the Women's Studies Center at Kaunas University of Technology (located in Kaunas, the second largest city in Lithuania), I quickly accepted. At that time, my knowledge of Lithuania was limited, but I was intrigued by the prospect of "watching history in the making." I was also excited about finally being able to teach "Women, the Law, and Social Policy," a subject close to my research interests.

I put together a course reader which included chapters from *Cinderella Goes to Market: Citizenship, Gender and Women's Movements in East Central Europe* by Barbara Einhorn (1993) and *Gender Politics and Post-Communism: Reflections from Eastern Europe and the Former Soviet Union*, a volume of essays written by women scholars in the post-Communist countries and edited by Nanette Funk and Magda Mueller (1993). The other course material was written by Western feminists.

After working our way through basic Western feminist theory, we started reading the literature about Communist and post-Communist women. My students, who had been rather shy, were excited to read the articles that spoke to them. They explained that this was their lives, but that they had never read anything like it before. Although nothing they read covered Lithuania specifically, it was their first feminist critiques of the experiences of Communist and post-Communist women.

We began discussing what kinds of things were available for them to read, and I discovered that very little had been published about Lithuanian women. There has never, to my knowledge, been a book published in English or Lithuanian that comprehensively described Lithuanian women and their lives.

As I learned about Lithuanian women and culture, my respect grew. Surely, the women of this tenacious nation merit their own voice. This manuscript is the fruition of that thought. I wanted to work on a project which would contribute to the women's studies program after I left the country, and compiling a book of essays about Lithuanian women seemed to be the perfect project. It was important to have the women scholars of the country write about their areas of expertise.

Some authors wrote in Lithuanian, and then had their essays translated, while some wrote in English. Language problems did exist, and this made the editing process difficult. Several meetings to clarify terms and ideas took place. I felt very sensitive about being an outsider, a Western feminist, imposing my views on the authors, and I sincerely tried to maintain the integrity of the authors' scholarship. They have agreed that this final version is what they wanted to say: their voice.

A grant application to have this manuscript translated into Lithuanian is in progress.

Suzanne LaFont

Acknowledgments

I would like to thank my students at Kaunas University of Technology. Their eagerness to learn inspired this project. In particular I would like to thank Dalia Gineitienė, Agnė Pankūnienė, and Renata Guobužaitė for their contributions. I would also like to thank all the other authors for their hard work and for their belief that this project would come to fruition.

This project would have never happened without the Civic Education Project. Hence, I am grateful to CEP for sending me to Lithuania and providing a supportive environment during my stay there. While in Lithuania, I had the pleasure to befriend Nandini Rajamdan. My stay, my research, this project, and my life have all been enriched by our friendship. Patricia Monahan and Michael Kaplan deserve special thanks for their patience and assistance during the early editing phase. The prepublication readers also offered valuable suggestions which improved this manuscript.

I would like to thank the many scholars before me who wrote so clearly about Communism and women—although their works did not apply directly to Lithuania, without them I could have never understood the woman/state dynamic of Soviet and post-Soviet Lithuania.

Very special thanks goes to Anders Peltomaa, my husband, who has helped me with every stage of this book. His advice, skills, wisdom, and patience were invaluable. Of course, any mistakes or errors remain solely my responsibility.

Introduction

Suzanne LaFont

> *Our women rule over many men: some in administering small rural districts, towns, and estates; others by making profit and still others through inheritance. These women rule, spurred on by passion, under the pretext of girlhood or widowhood, they lead unrestrained lives, pestering their subjects, they persecute some with their hatred, others because of blind love, they promote here, demote there.*
>
> —Secretary to the Grand Duchy of Lithuania, Mykolas Lietuvis, 1550.[1]

Anyone interested in Lithuanian women quickly learns three interesting facts. (1) In 1529, unique to "civilized" Europe, the First Statute of Lithuania (the legal code) ensured gentry women's inheritance and property rights; (2) When the Russians banned the Lithuanian press (1864–1904), brave Lithuanian women ran underground schools to keep the Lithuanian language alive; and (3) The most revered Lithuanian woman is the internationally famous archaeologist, the late Marija Gimbutas, whose research suggests that much of paleolithic Europe, including Lithuania, was populated by a nonpatriarchal, matristic culture. She is a national icon, and her theories are enthusiastically embraced by women scholars.

While these facts are interesting on their own, also noteworthy is the pride that surrounds the telling. Rather than focusing on prejudice and discrimination, Lithuanian women are quick to detail their contributions and strengths. They are eager to have their voices heard, tell their stories, and teach us about their culture. For the past fifty years, the identity of Lithuanian women has, to the outside world, been subsumed with that of Soviet women. Yet, Lithuanian women are different and proud of their differences. In this volume—the first ever published in English—we finally have the opportunity to learn about our Lithuanian sisters.

HISTORY

In 1990, after a civil uprising in which fourteen unarmed civilians were killed, Lithuania declared its independence from the Soviet Union. So began another era of independence for this small strategically located country.

Since its declaration of nationhood in 1236, Lithuania has been invaded by the Teutonic Order, the Russians, Napoleon, the Swedes, the Germans, and the Poles. However, far from being a passive European doormat, Lithuania established in the beginning of the fifteenth century an empire that extended almost all the way from the Baltic to the Black Sea. This feat inspired—and has helped maintain—immense pride in the Lithuanian national heritage through the many years of subsequent foreign invasions. In fact, prior to 1990, Lithuania experienced only twenty-five years of real independence during the last two hundred years.

Foreign occupation has always meant oppression and resistance, and, for this, many Lithuanians have paid the price. Between 1941–1953, the Russians deported more than one hundred thousand Lithuanians to Siberia and martyred Lithuanian forest freedom fighters who fought bravely for independence. All the attempts to destroy Lithuania, the country, the people, the language, and the culture have failed. The essays in this volume reveal that Lithuanian women share well-deserved credit for these failures and take immense pride in their roles in maintaining Lithuanian culture.

The first chapter of this volume, written by Dr. Viktorija Baršauskienė and Giedrė Rymeikytė, offers a historical overview of the role of women in Lithuania. They provide basic information about Lithuanian history. They trace women's educational and economic opportunities from thirteenth century to the Soviet takeover in the 1940s, and they discuss how wars shaped the status of Lithuanian women. We learn that Lithuania's frequent involvement in warfare has inadvertently had a positive impact on the role of women who gained power in the absence of men. Despite the high status which Lithuanian women held prior to the Soviet takeover, discrimination in education and employment predated communism, and the occupational segregation that solidified under Communist rule had its roots in precommunist Lithuania. Dr. Baršauskienė and Ms. Rymeikytė also discuss the rise of Lithuanian national pride. Indeed, the style of their essay demonstrates that pride. Their essay inspires appreciation for the hardships which Lithuanians have endured to retain their cultural identity, their language, and their lands. We begin to understand why this small country is so proud of their big heritage.

Approaching women's history from a different perspective, Dr. Dalia Vyšniauskienė writes in chapter 2 about Lithuanian women in literature. Her descriptions of the works and lives of women writers provides insights and depth to our knowledge about the role of women in precommunist Lithuanian culture. Through Dr. Vyšniauskienė's analysis of their works, we see the historical and symbolic meanings of womanhood. She demonstrates the ways in which literary topics have reflected—and continue to reflect—historical transformations. For example, the agrarian lifestyle made so precarious through war and foreign occupation is reflected in the many stories that are "rooted" to the land. Lithuania's women authors have, at times, mourned the urbanization processes that stripped them of their land. They write about modernization and the ensuing loss of traditional ways of life that leads to alienation and uncertainty. However, they also write about the freedoms to explore and question new lifestyles, sexual mores, and moral issues. Dr. Vyšniauskienė shows us the strengths of Lithuanian women and the hardships which they have endured through the lives of the nation's women authors and the women characters of those authors' books.

Chapter 3—*Life Histories: Three Generations of Lithuanian Women*—is written by a Kaunas University student, Agnė Pankūnienė. She writes about her grandmother's life, her mother's life, and her own life. Her heartfelt narrative offers a glimpse of the difficulties which Lithuania women faced prior to, during, and after the Soviet era. We learn about the demands of rural life, the hardships caused by deportations to Siberia, the transition from rural to urban life, the Soviet labor machinery, the ways in which social policies and day care impacted women's lives, the consequences of privatization, and their uncertainty about the future. These three life histories beautifully encompass the experience of

Lithuanian women and offer a sharp contrast to the way in which this period was once viewed by the Western feminists.

In the 1960s and 1970s, American feminists viewed Soviet women from afar and envied their situation. We read about the "protectionist" laws governing Soviet women—laws that provided three years of maternity leave; widely available, state-sponsored child care; and secure abortion rights. We thought we were seeing emancipation. It appeared that Soviet women had been given many of the things that we were fighting for. Pictures of women in hard hats, women technicians, and women doctors supported the illusion that women in the Communist countries had, indeed, been liberated.

Yet, rather than experiencing complete emancipation, Lithuanian women were forced into a pseudo emancipation, mainly because their labor was needed for Communist industrial development. The importance of women's role as the producers of future workers was recognized, while, at the same time, state ideology encouraged women's participation in the labor force and deprived housewifery of status (Korovushkina 1994). Work was a duty, not a right, and low wages necessitated both wives' and husbands' incomes for family survival. The equality that the Communist governments proclaimed translated into women working like men in the labor market. Importantly, no counter "equality" existed for men's involvement in the domestic domain. Pre-Communist patriarchy remained intact, with women shouldering the burden of economic and domestic labor. Instead of truly liberating women, state communism turned into a system that doubly exploited women in their roles as producers and reproducers.

Not surprisingly, Lithuanian women did not feel emancipated. They recount feeling exhausted—an understandable state for women who worked an average of seventy-two hours a week, at least five more hours a week than men did (United Nations Publications 1995). Lithuanian women experienced the same double burden that many women in other Communist nations experienced, that is working for paid employment and performing the majority of domestic duties—a task that increased significantly when shortages set in.

THE TRANSITION PERIOD

The collapse of the totalitarian regime has provided Lithuanian women with increased opportunities for dialogue and criticism on one hand, and, on the other, they are degraded in new ways through pornography and beauty contests (Pavilionienė 1995). Communism, at least, promised to liberate women through increased opportunities in education, employment, and political representation (Goldman 1993). It failed, because it neglected to eliminate patriarchy. Unfortunately, the introduction of the market economy and democracy holds no such promise.

Lithuanian women face many of the same problems as do other post-Communist women. The transition to a market economy has created many social and economic problems, such as growing unemployment, inflation, a decline in real wages, and general economic insecurity (Funk 1993).

Many of the same contradictions concerning the role of women are also apparent. At a glance the women of Lithuania are relatively homogenous. Eighty-one percent are ethnically Lithuanian, while the remaining 19 percent are predominately Russians and Poles. Diversity is apparent, however, in the growing discrepancy between the rich and the poor, and variations in lifestyles. It is not unusual to see young women with dyed blonde hair and heavy makeup wearing miniskirts, and tottering down "Main Street" in high heels. Currently, however, these Lithuanian Barbies might be sharing the walkways with young women who look like they came straight from Greenwich Village in New York City. These fashion statements contrast with that of many elderly women who are cloaked in babushkas, worn-out coats, and old woolen stockings. Regardless of age and attire, there is growing evidence that Lithuanian women are being disadvantaged in the post-Communist era (Andrisiunaitė 1995).

Chapters 4, 5, and 6—which discuss the familial, educational, and economic status of Lithuanian women—all suggest that equality, as defined by the Soviet government, has lingered, and is as fraudulent now as it was prior to 1990.

FAMILY, EDUCATION, AND LABOR MARKET

In chapter 4, Giedrė Purvaneckienė details the attitudes, beliefs and aspirations that Lithuanians hold regarding family life. She begins her essay with a history of women's roles in the family and the laws regarding her status. She points out that Christianity and Russian rule undermined the traditional high status of Lithuanian women. These influences were viewed as temporary setbacks, after which Lithuanian women renewed their high status in the family. Dr. Purvaneckienė discusses how important family is to Lithuanian women, and how important women's roles in the family has been to Lithuanian culture. Yet, despite the high status which women enjoy in the domestic domain, patriarchy has persisted in Lithuania.

Dr. Purvaneckienė's research reveals the conservative attitudes of both Lithuanian women and men regarding familial roles. Many women who were over-burdened during the Soviet years now long for the luxury of traditional family life with man as provider and woman as homemaker. Most women, however, do not have the option of being homemakers because households need two incomes. In lieu of staying home, Dr. Purvaneckienė's research identifies an ideal but seldom-realized work model for women which is based on their reproductive role. That is, women should work full-time prior to childbirth. After the birth of the first child, women should remain home until the child or children are of school age. Then, women should work part-time until the children leave home. At this point women should resume full-time employment.

However, given the current job market, this scenario seems unrealistic. It advocates that women leave the labor force, at least as full-time employees, for several years. Yet, rapid changes in technology and the competition fostered by the market economy mean that mothers who choose to stay home with their children will be qualified only for the lowest level of employment, if they can find employment at all.

Chapter 5, *Lithuanian Women and Education: Discrimination and Career Choices,* details Lithuanian women's status in the education system. We learn that Lithuanians are well-educated, and that women's enrollment in higher education exceeds men's enrollment. Despite this, women experience discrimination in academe, with most appointments to dean and full professorships being given to men. Palmira Jucevičienė argues that this discourages women from pursuing academic careers. Instead, women tailor their educational aspirations on realistic career choices. A sex-specific choice of studies occurs in Lithuania with women concentrated in education at both primary and secondary levels, and pre-medical, while most of the students at technical schools are men.

Patriarchy in the home also takes its toll on women's educational goals. Many women experience increased difficulties in graduate school because, by that time of their lives, they are already mothers and have to perform the majority of domestic duties within the household in addition to their studies. Thus begins the cycle of women's under-representation in positions of money and power. Men are free from domestic constraints to pursue advanced degrees and secure top positions, whereas women get lower-paying jobs because they are viewed as unreliable workers as their familial duties prevent them from being model employees. The communist government tried to address this issue but failed. Early communist social policies relating to women's reproductive role—as seen in maternity leave and the like—facilitated women's involvement in the labor market. Yet, they also reinforced women's traditional roles in the domestic domain by granting benefits to mothers and excluding fathers (Einhorn 1993).

Chapter 6, *Women and the Economy*, written by Vida Kanopienė, discusses the fact that Lithuanian women, like their Soviet sisters, did make inroads into traditionally male-dominated fields such as engineering, medicine, and higher education. Their employment rates reached 80 percent, a level unknown in the West. Despite this, sex segregation in the labor force persisted with women concentrated in the low-status, low-paying jobs, and being passed over for promotions and important positions because their childcare and domestic responsibilities prevented them from being reliable workers. Furthermore, as Dr. Kanopienė notes that, when women became concentrated in traditionally male professions—such as professors and doctors—the profession itself became feminized, and tended to lose both status and remuneration. For the most part, women were confronted with a highly sex-segregated job market which rewarded them with low status and low-paying employment. Most women worked in the caring and service fields, while male workers were concentrated in more valued fields of heavy industry, construction, and transportation. Education, health care, retail, and light industry were almost completely feminized.

Men dominated the top of the occupational pyramid during the Communist era, and that situation has not changed. The more competitive job market now threatens to inhibit women's potential to benefit from the transition from a command to a market economy. Dr. Jucevičienė's research in chapter 5 found that 40 percent of the women students she surveyed had personally experienced sexual discrimination in the job market. Newspapers have numerous sex-specific job advertisements. A glance at the "Help Wanted" section of local newspapers reveals that foreign joint ventures openly prefer men. Want ads specify, not only which sex is desired, but, when woman applicants are sought, the additional qualification of "attractive" is often added. The Lithuanian daily paper, *Lietuvos Rytas*, carried an advertisement placed by the Ministry of Transportation which sought women secretaries and male technicians. This is in direct conflict with the country's Constitution which has outlawed sex discrimination.[2]

Ironically, for young women, discrimination in the new job market is linked to the Communist legacy. Social entitlements which were designed to facilitate women's participation in the workforce are creating increased discrimination. Although the new Lithuanian constitution has made social entitlements gender neutral—for example, fathers are eligible for parental leave—it is usually mothers who take time off from work for child-care responsibilities. As the state begins to shift the economic burden of social entitlements to private industry, women, as potential mothers, become expensive to employ. Alina Žvinklienė (1995, 12) writes, "New social insurance clearly ensures women's unemployment, since opportunities in the private business sector have clearly decreased, especially for women who have small children, because the employer is not interested in paying women-mothers the social guarantees prescribed by the law."

Without the totalitarian state to enforce employment policies, there is a greater potential for them to be ignored or misused. Standard employment applications include questions related to age and marital status. As a group of graduating students had asked for my help in filling out applications for a foreign company operating in Lithuania, I remarked that employers in the United States were not allowed to ask about age and marital status. They stated that this was standard practice in Lithuania, and that young married women had difficulties securing employment from foreign and local companies. Later, an unemployment counselor explained to me that women are being asked by employers to sign contracts waiving their legal rights to employment benefits.

Given this scenario, it is not surprising that women's unemployment rates are increasing at an alarming rate. Dr. Kanopienė found that, in 1992, 62 percent of unemployed persons were women. Despite the dismal employment situation, it does not seem that women are abandoning the job market. The economic decline means that families continue to need two incomes for survival. This fact, coupled with the early, almost universal marriage at an average age of 22 and subsequent early childbearing, means that most mothers work. Lengthy maternity leaves however are available, with reduced compensation even though most families cannot afford the loss of income, and state-sponsored child-care centers are closing down or unaffordable. Basically, the new governments are shifting the economic burden of child care to unpaid labor in the home, and, in the vast majority of cases, it is women's unpaid labor.

As inequality in Lithuania grows very evident, winners and losers are emerging. The winners represent a very small elite group of successful entrepreneurs and those who profit from the "gray economy" that is the Lithuanian Mafia (Milanovic 1994). Given the urgency of the economic crisis, the needs of women as a specific group have been easily ignored. Particularly prone to poverty are single mothers and older women, and the largest percentage of unemployment is found in middle-aged or older women. The closer they are to pension age, the less desirable they are to employers. In addition, pensions are inadequate and sex-specific life longevity is pronounced in Lithuania, with women living on average eleven years longer than men (Lithuanian Department of Statistics 1994). Consequently almost all of the beggars I have seen in Lithuania—as well as Russia, Estonia and Poland—have been elderly women. The same dynamics that have created the feminization of poverty in the West are evolving in the post-Communist economies. Women without the strength, skills, determination, or time to participate in the struggle for resources and power soon might not have the safety net of the Soviet welfare system to catch them from falling into economic and political despair.

LITHUANIAN NATIONALISM

Nationalism has emerged in popular and political discourse as the new government tries to reestablish a national identity. Lithuania is proud and nostalgic of its pre-Communist history which is portrayed as a happier time without such problems as high divorce rates, unmarried mothers, and juvenile delinquency. Political propaganda, the media, and the church point to women's participation in the labor force as the cause of social ills, in contrast to the idealized pre-Communist era when women stayed at home and took good care of their children and husbands. The sentiment is that if women would only return to the family where they belong, this past period of supposed societal bliss could be recreated.

Dr. Purvaneckienė's research in chapter 4 reveals that the history of the pre-Communist eras is, indeed, being reinvented. Society was not free from the social ills found today, nor were women staying at home. The truth is that Lithuania was agricultural, and women worked alongside men in the fields until the Communist push for industrialization. The traditional family of man as provider and woman as homemaker never existed. The direct shift from agriculture to communism meant that the one-income family wage never developed.

Unfortunately, the Lithuanian sense of national pride is being manipulated by a small but vocal part of the population. In chapter 7, *The Church, Nationalism, and the Reproductive Rights of Women*, Dalia Gineitienė critiques the current rise in nationalism and what it means for Lithuanian women. She points out that the recent rise in nationalism and nostalgia for tradition has many serious consequences for women. For women, the dangers of nationalism are twofold. First, by emphasizing women's roles as the reproducers of future citizens, the conservative nature of nationalism relegates women to a secondary role in civil life. Second, by granting primacy to the importance of the ethno-nation, nationalism masks gender-based, as well as class-based, inequality.

The current push to return post-Communist women to the domestic domain is linked, not only to increased familial stability, but also to the need to increase birth rates. Slogans such as "We are a perishing nation" are popular. Fertility rates in Lithuania are low— 2.0 during the period of 1990–1995, it was 2.1 in the United States for this same period—and are well publicized (United Nations Publications 1995). Many of my students expressed concern over the fact that more people are dying than being born. The level of anxiety relating to this issue is such that policies are being promoted which would prohibit the adoption of Lithuanian orphans by foreigners, even if it meant that the child would be raised in an orphanage.

Young women who watched their mothers struggle with the double burden are being encouraged to see their devotion to motherhood and family as a solution to the nation's problems. In essence, the idea of returning women to the home kills two birds with one stone. With unemployment levels reaching record highs and birth rates reaching record lows, successfully persuading women to stay home and have children can superficially solve both problems simultaneously.

Some Lithuanians believe that one way to increase fertility is to outlaw abortions, consequently measures restricting abortions have been discussed. Ms. Gineitienė points out that the Catholic Church, the most powerful religious institution in Lithuania, sees this transition period as an opportunity to end abortion rights. It has sponsored public ceremonies mourning aborted fetuses as lost citizens. Nuns and church members parade down the streets holding candles representing lives lost to abortion. International organizations are also arriving on the scene and joining the Church's battle.

I myself attended two conferences relating to the issue of family and family planning in Lithuania. In September 1994, an International Right-to-Life conference was hosted at Vytautas University. The Catholic Bishop was the guest of honor, and speakers from the United States and Poland all spoke on the evils of abortions and pledged support to the Lithuanian right-to-life cause. The following month, a conference titled "Lithuanian Family: Traditions and the Future" was held at the parliament. The Prime Minister, the Bishop, a United Nations representative and others formed an all-male panel to discuss family issues. No one protested as the Lithuanian Catholic Bishop used this government-sponsored conference to argue for, not only a ban on abortion, but on all forms of birth control other than natural family planning. The pronatalism of the Church, conjoined with nationalist propaganda, creates a moral, spiritual and patriotic basis for reproduction.

Most women I talked to did not seem concerned about the anti-abortion movement. They felt that their abortion rights were so secure that there was no need to form an opposition. To place the abortion issue in context, we must remember that abortion was and remains the main form of birth control in Lithuania. With little or no sex education and lack of information and access to affordable contraception, abortion rates are high (eighty abortions for every one-hundred live births, in the United States there are thirty-four abortions per one-hundred live births) (Purvaneckienė 1994, World Wide Web 1997). In 1994, Dr. Purvaneckienė found that only 11 percent of the Lithuanian population (11 percent of the men and 10 percent of the women) thought that abortion should be totally banned, while 70 percent (68 percent of the men and 72 percent of the women) felt that abortion should not be restricted. Women's reproductive rights in Lithuania seem safe, at least for now.

WOMEN'S ACTIVISM

Lithuanian women have a history of being active in civil life. As early as 1907, women's organizations were campaigning for equal rights, and, when Lithuania declared independence from Russia in 1917, women petitioned for the vote, equal rights, and representation. They were granted the vote, equal rights and also elected six women to the Lithuanian Seimas or parliament of St. Petersburg (Voverienė

1995). When independence was established in 1920, the new Lithuanian constitution guaranteed equal legal rights for women and men. Women's roles in public life flourished until the Soviet takeover in 1940.

Under the Soviet regime, women were guaranteed 36 percent of the positions in the legislative body of the Supreme Soviet (Purvaneckienė 1994). Yet, the entire concept of representation during this period should be considered within the context of totalitarianism.

The quota system and the entire concept of representation has been severely criticized as misleading (Corrin 1994). Nevertheless, the post-Communist government has replaced the quota system with democratic elections. Not surprisingly, the number of women as elected and appointed officials has decreased dramatically. In 1994, only ten (7 percent) women were elected to the Seimas. This figure increased substantially in 1996 when twenty-four women (18 percent) were elected to the Seimas. The agenda of these new women politicians seems promising, as fourteen of the women elected have agreed to unite in efforts to address women's issues (Pavilionienė 1997).

Independence brought political prominence to at least one Lithuanian woman. In 1990, Dr. Kazimiera Prunskienė was appointed as the first woman Prime Minister. Her reign, however, was short-lived, and she resigned in 1991. Dr. Prunskienė considers herself to be an exception rather than part of a trend toward the acceptance of women in high office, and she complained that the male dominated Seima would not allow her to appoint any women ministers. She writes, "Having won independence, government posts became objects of competition, and the rules of the game changed. In seeking to win higher positions and to reinforce their influence, and monopolist positions, men started to form intrigues and to compromise me. Attempts were made aggressively and incorrectly to shove me out of political activity . . . " (Prunskienė 1995:16).

Now that the public sphere of politics and business is gaining in value, women are being assigned to the private sphere of the home. At the same time, the home which enjoyed a heightened value under communism as an antitotalitarian sanctuary is losing its guarded status. In other words, women were guaranteed representation when representation was little more than a formality, and, now that the political arena is being empowered, they are being poorly represented.

To counter male dominance in the Lithuanian government, Dr. Prunskienė and other involved women established the

Lithuanian Party of Women on 25 February 1995. Women politicians, such as Dr. Prunskienė, who did not want to align themselves with any of the existing political parties found that they could not run for elected office without a party affiliation. Hence, they formed the Lithuanian Party of Women. However, that party has not garnered enough support even among the small group of women espousing women's issues to make it a viable political force. Some women believe that the party can never again enough popularity to make it a real force in politics, nor can it challenge the existing male-dominated political machinery. Other women believe that the party will serve only to further divide women, many of whom, already have firm loyalties to another party. During the 1996 elections, the women's party captured less than 5 percent of the vote, but Dr. Prunskienė was elected as an independent candidate. At this point the future of the women's party seems uncertain.

In chapter 8, Dalia Teišerskytė, chairman of the Lithuanian Party of Women council, details the reasons why the party was formed. Her testament—a heartfelt plea for the betterment of women—is an example of perhaps the largest school of thought regarding women's roles. She argues that Lithuanian men have handled the running of the country very poorly, and that women, who are the backbone of society, can transform politics into a harmonious forum supporting women and men together. She also quotes many different women's ideas about what's happening with Lithuanian women today. Their views run the gamut from prolife to poststructural perspectives. Ms. Teišerskytė's essay is at once idealistic and inspirational.

In chapter 9, Marija Pavilionienė critiques the Lithuanian Party of Women's platform and political strategies. Her criticism, in addition to being insightful, also illustrates a lack of consensus among women in terms of political empowerment. It seems that Lithuanian women do have something in common with their Western sisters—namely lack of consensus regarding women's roles.

With reproductive rights being threatened, wide-spread sex discrimination in the labor market leading to women's higher unemployment rates, and lack of a voice in the new governments, it would seem that Lithuanian women would be organizing to counteract these trends. Yet, the Lithuanian women's movements are poorly supported. The reasons for this are complex and relate to a combination of social, political, and economic factors.

Rejecting the idea of Communist equality is seen by some women as liberating (Petrova 1994). My experience in teaching women's studies in Lithuania supports this idea.

During my first lecture on Western feminist theory, after a few minutes of murmuring among my students, one student raised her hand and asked, "So, we are wondering, who is more liberated.[2] The woman who works, or the woman who stays at home?" They felt that having the choice to stay home was liberating. Remember that, to them, work was a duty, not a right, and that the patriarchal division of labor in the household persisted. Thus, women who have the option of being oppressed by two systems—domestic patriarchy and the discriminatory labor market—or by only one system of patriarchy, could certainly construe staying home as liberating. For many women, opposing the patriarchal division of labor in the home was not perceived as being possible or even desirable.

Nationalism also inhibits a women's movement. Unlike many of the other communist countries—such as Hungary, Poland, and Bulgaria—that retained formal independence, Lithuania was incorporated into the Soviet Union. Their church and national identity were suppressed. Currently, everything Lithuanian is valued because it is not Soviet. Criticizing the new Lithuania is wrong because it is unpatriotic. Consequently, the Lithuanian women's movement seems to be inhibited by love of nation. Most women identify with other groups—most prominently the ethno-nation—before they identify as women in terms of group interests. Their role as citizens is to build the national image.

I was invited to speak at a women's club in Kaunas. On the way to the meeting, I was discussing one of my student's research with my colleague. The topic was rape, and my student had found a high incidence of rape and attempted rape among university students. At the meeting, my colleague brought this up. Some of the women seemed interested but one visibly upset woman burst out shouting that she did not believe a word of it, and, furthermore, this type of discussion was not the intended purpose of their club. It was as if Lithuanian men could not possibly be rapists. The subject was quickly replaced with the need to distribute Christmas presents to local prisoners.

Women who take an interest in women's issues are at risk of being labelled feminists. The entire concept of feminism has been discredited with the term being misunderstood and associated with the most extreme of Western feminists. The Lithuanian stereotype of a Western feminist is a masculine, domineering woman who hates men. Although many women lead their lives in ways which most Western feminists would label as liberated—that is, obtaining high education, achieving economic independence, and valuing their careers—most post-Communist women are reluctant to use the term. For example, when one of the founders of the Lithuanian Party of Women told me she would be visiting New York City, I offered to put her in contact with politically active American feminists. She vehemently responded that she was not interested in meeting any feminists.

Even the role and direction of the Women's Studies Centres at Vilnius, Kaunas, and Klaipėda Universities is unclear. The Women's Studies Centre at Vilnius was set up and runs in the Western classic model of Women's Studies which focuses on Western feminist discourse and theory. The Women's Studies at Kaunas University offers more practical how-to courses such as "Women and a Healthy Life," and "Women in Business." A small group of women debate the concept of correct feminism, and an even smaller group discusses the concept of feminist imperialism. Regardless of the adapted or adopted feminist model, the important issue is the fact that this small country already has three departments, which is an impressive accomplishment.

Lithuanian feminists often point out the stages through which the Western feminist movement went to reach its current level, and they suggest that post-Communist feminism is in its infancy. The privileged origins of the Western feminist movement is so different from what Communist women experienced that they cannot relate to it. In fact, the very language of feminism is not necessarily found in Lithuanian. The English word gender has no translatable counterpart, and sexual harassment is not translatable linguistically, although the act itself was very well-known. Even the concepts of equality, justice, and liberation have been revised to fit into the Communist discourse. Many ideas and concepts are tossed about and inadequately defined or understood. It is clearly going to take some time to clear the smoke, breakdown the stereotypes, redefine or mutually reconstruct the meaning of many concepts and ideas.

In chapter 9, Dr. Pavilionienė details the inception of the Women's Study Centre at Vilnius University, and she discusses the trials and tribulations of its short history. The Centre suffers from lack of funding, faculty, and books. It has been assigned a low priority within the university system, and insecurity concerning the future is a constant reality.

In addition to the political arena and Women's Study Centres, Lithuanian women are active in many ways. There are currently thirty-three women's organizations operating in the country. Several women scholars are members of East/West Network of Women, an on-line forum for post-Communist and Western feminists. Lithuanian women also attended the United Nations' Beijing Conference in 1995, and they compiled a report on the status of women in Lithuania for that conference. A _Woman's World_ newsletter is published a few times each year, detailing women's activities and highlighting information and research concerning women. Members of the Women's Study Centre were successful in their recommendations that the Open Society Fund translate some feminist classics into Lithuanian, and a few titles are now available. The Vilnius Women's Home—the first abused women's shelter—has received funding, and will soon be operational. Numerous seminars and conferences relating to women's issues have been held in Lithuania, and Lithuanian women have been able to attend many international conferences. The Nordic countries have been most forthcoming with funds and guest lecturers to fill in when projects run short, and Lithuanian women express thanks for having such liberated sisters nearby. In 1995, Lithuania ratified the United Nations Convention Against the Elimination of All Forms of Discrimination Against Women.

Recognition of the importance of women's issues has a long way to go, and setbacks do occur. In 1995, the Women's Study Centre at Kaunas lost its annual Civic Education visiting lecturer position because the department decided to concentrate on business studies instead. In March 1997, the new government abolished the position of State Counselor on Women's Issues of the Republic of Lithuania, which had been held by Dr. Purvaneckienė, the authors of chapter 4 of this book. This was a special post-Communist position created to address women's issues. Now that it has been eliminated, women have no special voice in the upper government. Prostitution, violence against women, rape, and pornography sales are also all on the rise (Litvinaitė 1996).

As discouraging as all of these facts are, it does seem that Lithuanian women are standing strong and making progress. Renata Guobužaitė's essay, _Modern Women in Lithuania: Finding Their Way_, which appears as chapter 10 in this book, represents the new generation of women. Twenty-two-year-old, Guobužaitė writes about the dilemmas facing young women. The East/West dichotomy with which they are now confronted leaves women wondering about their future and how to incorporate their history and culture into the new society. Superficially, independence has brought new freedoms and choices, but the current economic realities could actually reduce their choices and options. The transition has left many young women feeling as if they lack role models to help them find their way.

This volume ends with a tribute to Marija Gimbutas. Joan Marler's essay, *Marija Gimbutas: Tribute to a Lithuanian Legend*, details Dr. Gimbutas's life and career. Dr. Gimbutas's popularity is such that many of the contributors thought that this book should begin with this tribute. I resisted their suggestions with the hope that any reader unfamiliar with Dr. Gimbutas's work would further appreciate her life and work by first understanding her cultural heritage. Dr. Gimbutas' importance to women is twofold.

First, the international recognition she received for her research and writings is a success story which is inspirational to all women. Second, the subject of her research—identifying the importance of women in prehistory—appeals to women immensely. We are given a glimpse into the life of this extraordinary woman, her struggles, her triumphs, and her love of country.

CONCLUSION

Prior to independence, the Communist Party partially defined and redefined the role of Lithuanian women based on the demographic and labor-force needs of the Communist state. It accomplished this through propaganda, social policies, and the fact that incorporation into the social welfare system was dependent on workforce participation. It also had the power to enforce social policies, welfare benefits, and maintain child-care centers.

The quality of state-sponsored child care and the reality of benefits have been widely criticized. Yet, many policies, such as lengthy maternity leaves, were ideologically more progressive and generous than similar benefits afforded to American women. The bottom line is that these policies did offset some of the inequalities that existed in the domestic domain, and they eased the double burden somewhat.

Today, many of the social policies relating to Lithuanian women's employment remain intact. Dismantling the Communist state means that there has been a transfer of tasks and power from the government to the market. Without the totalitarian state to enforce social policies, they have the potential to be ignored or misused. In fact, retaining such policies during this period of dramatic economic reform appears to be having a negative impact on

Lithuanian women. As the state begins to shift the economic burden of social policies to private industry, policies designed to facilitate women's participation in the workforce, can actually increase discrimination. Women, as potential mothers, become expensive to employ.

Enforcement of rights, policies, and equality have all taken a back seat to the market economy, and that economy is becoming increasingly male dominated. The threat is nothing short of the devolution of women's rights. The role of the state is to ensure the rights and well-being of its citizens, but the market has no such social conscience. The goal of the state should be to enforce existing laws and policies which protect women's participation in the labor force, not to stand aside as they are eroded by the force of the market economy.

It is unlikely that women's interests will ever be thoroughly addressed in the male-dominated Lithuanian government. For women to be fully integrated, they must have a voice in the government to protect their interests, as well as appropriate legislation protecting their participation in the labor market and facilitating their double role as reproducers and producers. Yet, the state must have resources, desire, and power to enforce such policies.

The Communist government alternatingly denied or ignored women's inequality at work and at home. The new government seems to be taking a similar stand by concluding that the women's question will be solved later, when economic and political stability are achieved. Once this has happened, however, the women's question will already have been answered. Society will have been reorganized, leaving women behind.

The Lithuanian experience proves that the Communist model of simply increasing women's employment rates and political representation is insufficient for ending the oppression of women. The Communist and post-Communist experience of women has the potential to make a significant contribution toward understanding the dynamics of women's roles as producers and reproducers. Different countries in the world have employed different strategies to address this complex issue, but none have succeeded. Even the "woman-friendly" Scandinavian states have failed to completely eliminate those structural forces in society which produce inequalities between women and men (Siim 1993).

Ideologically, Communism created a space for equality, the current democracy should provide greater personal freedoms. A marriage of the two could produce new solutions regarding the empowerment of women. This is clearly a crucial time for Lithuanian women. We in the West can try to learn from their experiences, and hope that the double burden has not left them too tired to teach us what they have learned in one of the largest experiments with social engineering in modern history.

NOTES

1. This quote is taken from Mykolas Lietuvis's political treatise, *Concerning Customs of Tartars, Lithuanians and Muscovities*. It is quoted in "Woman's status in the Society of the Grand Duchy of Lithuania in the Sixteenth Century," by Dr. Irena Valikonytė, in *Lithuania: Women in the Changing Society*, a report compiled by Lithuanian nongovernmental organizations for the United Nations' Fourth Women's Conference in Beijing, 1995.

2. The Lithuanian language does not allow for gender neutral nouns, so gender neutral advertisements could become awkward or lengthy. However, there was no doubt that they wanted women secretaries and men technicians.

REFERENCES

Andrisiunaitė, Aurelija
    1995. *Women's Employment in the Domestic Domain*. Unpublished Masters thesis, Kaunas University of Technology, Kaunas, Lithuania.

Corrin, Chris
    1994. "Women's Politics in Europe in the 1990s." *Women's Studies International Forum*, 17:2(289–297). New York: Pergamon Press.

Einhorn, Barbara
    1993. *Cinderella Goes to Market: Citizenship, Gender and Women's Movements in East Central Europe*. New York: Verso.

Funk, Nanette
    1993. "Introduction" in *Gender Politics and Post-Communism: Reflections from Eastern Europe and the Former Soviet Union*, edited by Nanette Funk and Magda Mueller. 1–14. New York: Routledge.

Goldman, Wendy Z.
    1993. *Women, the State and Revolution: Soviet Family Policy and Social Life, 1917–1936*. New York: Cambridge University Press.
Kanopienė, Vida
    1995. "Women in the Labor Market" in *Lithuania: Women in the Changing Society*. 21–22, Vilnius: United Nations Development Program.

Korovushkina, Irina
1994. "Gender Equality under Real Socialism: Women and their Careers
in the USSR (1930–1960s)" in *Women in History—Women's History:
Central and Eastern European Perspectives*, edited by Andrea Peto
and Mark Pittaway. 99–106, Budapest: Central European University.

Lithuanian Department of Statistics
1994. *Lithuanian Women*. Vilnius, Lithuania.

Litvinaitė, Irena
1996. "Our Combined Efforts will Stop Violence." *Woman's World:
Newsletter of the Lithuanian Women's Issues Information Centre.*
3:10. Vilnius: United Nations Development Program.

Milanovic, Branco
1994. "A Cost of Transition: 50 Million Poor and Growing Inequality"
in *Transitions*, 5:8. Washington, D.C.: World Bank Publication.

Pavilionienė, Marija Aušrinė
1995. "Woman's Rights-Human Rights" in *Lithuania: Women in the
Changing Society*. 6–7, Vilnius: United Nations Development Program.
1997. Personal e-mail communication. 7 February 1997.

Petrova, Dimitrina
1994. "What Can Women Do to Change the Totalitarian Cultural Context?" in *Women's Studies International Forum*. 17:2. New York:
Pergamon Press.

Prunskienė, Kazimiera
1995. "I was regarded as an exception" in *Lithuania: Women in the
Changing Society*. 16. Vilnius: United Nations Development Program.

Purvaneckienė, Giedrė
1994. *Women's World*, the newsletter of the Lithuanian Preparatory
Committee of the IV World Conference on Women. Vilnius: United
Nations Development Program.

Siim, Birte
1993. "The Gendered Scandinavian Welfare States" in *Women and Social
Policies in Europe*, edited by Jane Lewis. 25–48. Hants, England:
Edward Elgar Publishers.

United Nations Publications
1995. *The World's Women 1995: Trends and Statistics*. New York.

Valikonytė, Irena
1995. "Women's Status in the Society of the Grand Duchy during the
Sixteenth Century" in *Lithuania: Women in the Changing Society*.
8–9. Vilnius: United Nations Development Program.

Voverienė, Ona
   1995. "Women's Movement in Lithuania: Historical Background" in
   Lithuania: Women in the Changing Society. 9–14, Vilnius: United
   Nations Development Program.

World Wide Web
   1997.   http://maxweber.hunter.cuny.edu/socio/kuechler/309/
   abo.stat.html1

Žvinklienė, Alina
   1995. "The 'New Right' Ideology in Lithuanian" in *Lithuania: Women
   in the Changing Society.* 11–12. Vilnius: United Nations Development Program.

Chapter 1

A Historical Perspective on the Role of Women

Viktorija Baršauskienė and Giedrė Rymeikytė

BASIC FACTS ABOUT LITHUANIA

The Republic of Lithuanian is located in the geographic center of Europe. Its western border is the Baltic Sea. Lithuania's other borders are shared in the north with Latvia, in the southeast with Belarus, and in the southwest with Poland and the Kaliningrad region of the Russian Federation. Lithuania covers an area of 25,200 square miles which is slightly larger than Switzerland or West Virginia.

Lithuania is a sovereign democratic state. Our new constitution was adopted on 11 March 1990. In 1994, the population of Lithuania was 3,724,000, and its capital, Vilnius, has a population of 542,000.

The official language is Lithuanian, which is the oldest of the living Indo-European languages. The country is predominately Roman Catholic.

THE HISTORY OF LITHUANIAN WOMEN

In this chapter, we examine the history of women in Lithuania. A historical perspective will help us understand and analyze the current status of Lithuanian women. It will also allow us to examine the perpetuation of women's oppression.

In prehistory, Finno-Ugric tribes inhabited the area of present Lithuania. Tribal women gathered food, developed agriculture, modeled pots, spun, and prepared food. It has been suggested that matriarchy was the form of social organization, with the mother as the head of the family and the tribe, and descent and kinship traced through the her (Dundulienė 1990). Around the fifth century B.C., Lithuania was invaded by Indo-European tribes who were agriculturalists, cattle breeders and had mastered iron. They brought to Lithuania a new form of social organization—namely, patriarchy.

The date most widely accepted as the formation of the Lithuanian state is A.D. 1236. The state was formed from many separate tribes including Aukštaičiai, Žemaičiai, Sėliai, Narduviai, Žiemgaliai, Skalviai, and Sūduviai. These tribes merged to defend their lands from the aggression of the Teutonic and Livonian German Orders who were more interested in controlling land than spreading Christianity (Ivinskis 1978). While the men were fighting, many women were left behind to manage the affairs of the farms and family. Thus, this period raised the level of involvement of women's socioeconomic activities.

The aggression intensified in the latter half of the thirteenth century and the fourteenth century. To end the invasions, Lithuania converted to Christianity in 1387. This conversion invalidated the claims of the Teutonic Order, and put an end to its war against Lithuania (Šapoka 1989). Inclusion into the Christian world spurred an intense period of economic and cultural development, along with orientation and integration into the Western world.

The fifteenth and sixteenth centuries were noted for increases in agriculture, population growth, and an increase in the number and size of towns. Book printing and the foundation of institutes of higher learning—such as Vilnius University—helped spread the ideas of humanism and the Reformation. During this period, the Lithuanian Codes of Law were established. These factors contributed to the consolidation of Lithuanian culture.

The growth of towns and the rise of trade prompted women's involvement in urban factories. There was, however, not much difference between women's work in the cities and in the countryside. Urban women were engaged in agricultural labor on small plots just outside the towns, and both urban and rural women worked in handicrafts (TSR 1985). Women's economic activities during this period were not significantly different from women's activities in other Eastern European countries.

In contrast to other European women, Lithuanian women's property rights were protected by the law. In feudal society, status was determined by class origin and property. There was a closed class of nobility and serfdom in Lithuania. Customs and traditions which defended the rights of women suggests that Lithuanian women enjoyed some economic independence. It was uncommon in feudal societies to legislate an official status for women. Yet when we examine the statutes of Lithuania, we find that gentry women had the right to inherit a part of their families' property. However, a gentry woman's rights were not the same as for sons. Daughters were entitled to smaller inheritances than were sons. Gentry women who were landowners had the right to many landowner privileges, even if they were not full-fledged members of the nobility. In addition, the Lithuanian statutes have chapters which carried sentences for beating or killing a woman which were double that for killing a man. It is believed that these laws reflect customary laws, and this implies that the status of Lithuanian women was high in contrast to other European countries during this period.

Class played a major role in determining women's economic behaviors. While lower-classed women worked in factories and on farms, women from the upper classes led very different lives. In the early 1800s, the lives of gentry women were discussed in the newspapers. Their main responsibility was to make their husbands' lives pleasant.

THE GROWTH OF INDUSTRY AND CAPITALISM

At the beginning of the seventeenth century, about 85 percent of the population were peasants, 8 percent were nobility, 6 percent were industrial laborers, and .04 percent were merchants. Women's economic activity outside of agriculture was greatest in small industries. Women worked primarily in industries which involved handwork, such as textiles and food production. The first industrial factory created in the early 1700s were owned by a woman named Ona Sanguškaitė-Radvilienė Šapoka 1989). This factory produced mirrors, ceramics, and tapestries.

Fewer women than men attended school during this period. In 1804, about 10 percent of the school population was girls. There were no state schools for girls, only boarding schools. Secondary schools were founded by monasteries and, as a consequence, were the domain of men. Thus, it was socially unacceptable for women to attend secondary school. This attitude began to change in the beginning of the nineteenth century. The education of rural girls, however, continued to be limited because their labor was needed on the farms, and because most schools were located in towns. By the end of the nineteenth century, 18 percent of the school students were girls. Women did not attend universities during this period.

In 1795, a large portion of Lithuania came under control of the Russian Empire. This annexation was met with resistance and rebellions to restore independence. Uprisings in 1794, 1830–1831, and 1863 were successfully suppressed. To prevent further uprisings, oppressive measures were taken. A policy of Russification was enforced, Vilnius University was closed, and the Lithuanian press was banned. Extra taxes were imposed on Catholic landowners—but not on Protestants—and an increasing number of peasants became serfs. After the abolition of serfdom in 1861, a market economy gradually took root. Lithuanian farmers grew richer, and their sons were educated, thus increasing the number of intellectuals of peasant descent. This led to the growth of a Lithuanian nationalist movement.

During the nineteenth century, women's work activities increased. They were involved in leather, textiles, wood, and metal industries (Lietuvos Istorijos Šaltiniai 1955). In 1894, 41 percent of the workers in the textile industry were women. Sixty-three percent of these workers were younger than 20 years of age. Working conditions in the textile industry were harsh, as the work was difficult and the factories were unsanitary. The predominance of young women in the labor force relates to the Lithuanian tradition that a woman works until she is married. Then, she leaves her job and stays home.

There were very few women white-collar workers. In 1897, 17 percent of white-collar workers were women, and, of these, most were teachers, lower-level health-care workers, clerks, and child-care workers. The feminization of these positions persists even today.

WOMEN DURING LITHUANIAN INDEPENDENCE OF 1918–1940

World War I and occupation by the German army in 1915 seriously damaged Lithuanian agriculture and industry. Agriculture was the most important part of Lithuania's economy with industry being of secondary importance. By the time the war was over and independence was restored, both were almost totally destroyed.

The new government began land reform in 1918. In comparison with Western Europe and the other Baltic States, Lithuania's land reform efforts were inefficient because of the vast number of small farms. More than 53 percent of the farms covered less than ten hectares, and an additional 30 percent were between ten and twenty hectares. Rural women either owned farms or were hired agricultural workers. Women farmers were disadvantaged by lack of technology, and the larger more advanced farms were owned by men (Jablonskis 1979).

Women were also disadvantaged in industry. Female participation in white-collar work was lower than that of men in all districts of Lithuania. Women constituted 41 percent of the blue-collar workers, but only 21 percent of the white-collar workers.

The most noted form of discrimination against women is found by analyzing wage tables. In 1930, unskilled women were paid only 58 percent of the wages unskilled men earned. As the years passed, however, this wage gap decreased, and, by 1938, women's wages were 72 percent of men's pay (Greimas 1993).

Work benefits for women were also limited. The 1925 Patient Law granted women eight weeks maternity leave—beginning two weeks before the child's birth and ending six weeks afterwards—and an allowance of fifty litas (the Lithuanian currency) or twenty days' wages.

From 1918 to 1949, the difference between Lithuanian girls' and boys' attendance at primary and secondary school was insignificant. As Lithuania's standard of living increased, the number of children attending school increased, and, hence, the number of teachers increased. In 1929, 47 percent of the teachers were women. This figure rose to 60 percent by 1939. The number of girls attending school also increased. In 1929, 43 percent of the primary school children were girls. This figure rose to 49 percent in 1939. A similar situation occurred in secondary schools. Although girls were well-represented in primary and secondary schools, the number of women attending the universities remained low. Women's participation in law, technical subjects, and theology was very low, whereas, in the humanities and medicine, women constituted almost half of the student body.

CONCLUSION

Historically, the status of women in Lithuania has been influenced by political, economic, religious, and social factors. Lithuania's history of war and foreign regimes has, on one hand, heightened women's status by fostering their independence in the absence of men. On the other hand, early Russian reign undermined women's legal rights, and religion had the effect of lowering women's status as Lithuania shifted from paganism to Christianity.

Lithuanian women have been economically active for centuries, but their involvement in the workforce was prompted by industrialization and the Soviet machinery. Their concentration in low-status and low-paying jobs began before the Soviet takeover, and persisted throughout the Communist years. The image of what women should be has evolved and changed many times, but patriarchy has persisted and inhibited women's ability to realize their full potential.

As we approach a new era, a new independence, and a new world environment, we hope that women's lives will improve, and that Lithuanian women will move forward with strength and determination.

REFERENCES

Dunduliené, P.
  1990. *Senovés Lietuviu, Mitologija ir Religija*. Vilnius.

Greimas, A. J.
  1993. *Lietuva Pabaltiji*. Vilnius.

Ivinskis, Z.
  1978. *Istorija Lietuvos*. Roma.

Jablonskis, K.
  1979. *Istorija ir Jos Šaltiniai*. Vilnius.

LIŠ
  1955. *Lietuvos Istorijos Šaltiniai*. Vilnius.

Šapoka, A.
  1989. *Lietuvos Istorijos*. Vilnius: Red Publishers.

TSR
  1985. *Lietuvos TSR Istorija*. Vilnius: Mokslas Publishers.

Chapter 2

Women in History and Literature

Dalia Vyšniauskienė

Lithuanian women have traditionally held a comparably high social position in society, and they have held an importance place in Lithuanian literature. However, the persistence of heathenism in Lithuania created a social status for women which was different from the Christian nations of Europe. This is evident, not only in literature, but also from historical records.

Lithuanian women were not enslaved by Christian dogma, laws, and traditions. The heathen images of "woman as mother" and "woman as hearth keeper" from national mythology are an important part of the Lithuanian heritage, and they have never completely given way to the Christian concepts of "woman as sinner." This distinguishes Lithuanian women from the neighboring Slavonic and Germanic nations.

The portrayals of women in Lithuanian literature differed from that of other European women during the Romantic Period by their independent reasoning, action, and activity. They had none of the complexes that Byron's women suffered from, nor the sentimentalism of George Sand's characters. Their romances led to happy married lives. They were capable of opposing men, and their opposition did not cause negative consequences. For example, the female character Grazina, not her husband, became a military leader. Aldona risked going to an enemy military camp to look for her beloved Konrad Valenrod.

These fictional heroines created interest in real historical figures of the Grand Principality of Lithuania, which was part of the Polish Kingdom in eastern Rzeczpospolita. Lithuanian history also has an abundance of real life women heroines. Pajauta, the daughter of the last high priest in pagan Lithuania, was involved in state politics. Birutė, the mother of Vytautas the Great, become one of most popular personalities of Lithuanian history. The daughter of Vytautas, Sofia, was a prominent wife of the Russian Tsar, Vasilij the Blind, and was sainted in the Russian Orthodox Church. The nineteenth-century rebel hero, Emilia Plater, fought against the Russian occupation and became popular among European romantic nationalists.

The turbulent history of the Grand Principality of Lithuania from the thirteenth through the eighteenth centuries, with its long-lasting wars, resulted in a marriage of Catholic dogma and heathen morals. The duty and death of young warriors was common throughout this period. Women endured long periods without Lithuanian men. They ruled the family and the household, and they lived under the constant threat of abuse and slavery. The norms in Lithuania were not the same as were those in Poland, even though they were united into one kingdom. Lithuanian women had more rights and freedoms. They could marry either Catholic or Orthodox men after the rites of baptism. They were free to manage a portion of their own property and dispose of their inheritance, even after marriage. Whereas a widow in Poland was obliged to mourn and could not remarry for a year, a Lithuanian widow could remarry in six months. Widows in Lithuania could also choose a new husband from a wide circle of men, including servants.

J. Cerasin, a well-known Polish lawyer of the sixteenth century, wrote about the differences between Polish and Lithuanian women in the following way:

> In our country women are like children in their families, they can have meals only when allowed by their husbands, they own estates and treasures, but remain real beggars, as everything is in the hands of the master husband, and he can, God bless him, deprive his wife of the last bite of bread. . . . But in the Principality [Lithuania] women are entitled to loan money to their husbands. They can sponsor activities and ransom prisoners of war. The rights of women differ in these two states which are ruled by one King. (Lowmianski 1949)

The relatively independent status of Lithuanian women with respect to their property led to a more independent status regarding their lifestyle choices. There was much gossip and uproar in Europe about the free sexual habits in our Principality (the Grand Principality of Lithuania). References to this behavior are found in the records of Pope Nuncial and in traveler's log-books. Christian morality, which considered sex to be a sin, was certainly violated in the country. To foreigners, even women's property rights were an outrage, because they were illegal in other countries.

Despite advanced legal rights and a revered social status, women's involvement in nontraditional activities met with public disapproval. Women involved in public activity faced possible condemnation and misunderstanding. As a result, women writers were forced to use pseudonyms.

As late as the beginning of the twentieth century, around 51 percent of the Lithuanian population was still illiterate. The small percentage (less than 2 percent) that studied in gymnasiums and universities were from the denationalized noblemen and rural petty bourgeoisie who spoke primarily Polish. Most graduates from official schools chose to study theology, medicine, or law at European universities, and few of them returned to the motherland. This contributed to the growing insulation of Lithuania from European influences, including literature. Consequently, there was a lack of educated Lithuanian-speaking leaders at the beginning of the growth of nationalism in this century.

LITHUANIAN WRITERS

Early Lithuanian prose was strongly influenced by Polish, Russian, and German literature, and inherited the methods and the social ideology of realism, often known as "Polish Positivism." Polish was the mother-tongue of most of the Lithuanian intelligentsia, and Lithuanian was their second language. The Polish press and language was never banned, and Polish literature was experiencing its golden age, enjoying such authors as I. Kraszewski, E. Orzeszkowa, B. Prus, H. Senkiewich (Nobel Prize winner 1905), and W. Reymont (Nobel Prize winner 1924).

Lithuanian writers of the late nineteenth century came from both the gentry and new country bourgeoisie, and they had various levels of education. Their nationalistic sentiments prompted the development of Lithuanian literature and helped standardize the Lithuanian language. Their writings have also played a very important role in the national movement. Created under censorship and printed abroad, Lithuania newspapers and books were a tool of resistance to the hegemony of Russian Empire. Some authors, including

the classic female authors, devoted their very lives to it. Nationalist supporters—called the "Litvomans"—were neither numerous
nor rich. Hence, most writers had to hold other jobs for financial
support. These factors influenced the quality of literature. To illustrate, S. Kymantaitė disparagingly called *Varpas,* the main
Lithuanian newspaper of the nineteenth century, "readings for the
lower classes."

WOMEN WRITERS

The high status of Lithuanian women resulted in a group of
important women authors in the nineteenth century. Six women
stand firmly in the history of both art and social life: Žemaitė; Bitė;
two sisters, Sofija and Marija Ivanauskaitė, who wrote together
under the name of Lazdynų Pelėda; Šatrijos Ragana; and S.
Kymantaitė. Although of very different talents, interests, and education, these women were all important activists in literature, and
their life stories illustrated the fate of women in Lithuanian history.

Žemaitė (1845–1921) was the most popular woman author of
the period. She was educated primarily in the home of relatives
where she mastered Lithuanian. She spent many years with her
husband, J. Žymantas, doing farm work while cherishing the hope
of a creative future. She started writing only after her children were
grown, and she had acquired property. Her rich life experiences
became the plots of her stories, and her gifts for storytelling and
vivid language are the hallmarks of her literature. Her talent earned
her recognition and awards, but her works were nationalist only in
a narrow sense. They are documents of everyday life, realistic portrayals of the social inequalities of the peasants in the province of
Kaunas. In her stories, people speak and act rather than reason. The
impacts of their actions are simple and easy to define. Žemaitė
never analyzed. She simply described life in a precise manner. This
authenticity gave life to her work. The documentary style of
Žemaitė, especially when she describes women and their status in
the family, is richer than any explanation or interpretation.

One of her typical stories, "Daughter-in-Law," describes three
women living in the same rural patrilocal conditions. According to
village tradition, daughters-in-law had low status in their husbands'
families, and their lives were often harsh. The older women, Drižienė
and Vingienė, had endured the "new family" periods, yet they
survived. Eventually, they attained status in their husbands' families. But Katrė, the third woman, was unprepared to fight for her-

self. She was not ready to be a housewife, yet she shows no aggression, just obedience. Of interest is Žemaitė's attitude toward Katrė. She shows sympathy, but no mercy.

Žemaitė left no large works, and her writings remain in the shadow of such novels as W. Reymont's *Peasants*, published in 1914, which was devoted to similar lifestyle descriptions, and was awarded the Nobel Prize in 1924. The works of Žemaitė were typical for an emerging national literature. In the course of time, they became interesting for other nations only as documents of life.

In contrast to Žemaitė, whose characters operated in action, the characters of Lazdynų Pelėda (the sisters Sofija [1867–1926] and Marija Ivanauskaitė [1872–1957]) confront emotional and moral dilemmas such as the economic and moral decline of landlords, economic inequality, selfishness, and other vices. The works of Pelėda are more important in social commentary than are those of Žemaitė.

Šatrijos Ragana (M. Pečkauskaitė 1877–1930) spent her childhood in artistic surroundings, and was educated and introduced to modern ideas of literature in Switzerland. She explored the methods of European Literature in Lithuanian, and became one of the first professional female teachers and self-supporting women. Ragana had a dynamic personality, and continued her education throughout her life.

The *Old Manor*, one of her famous works, is a radical expose of her social and aesthetic views of Lithuanian and Polish nationalism. All of Ragana's characters are strong individuals capable of both decision and of action. One of her heroines, Viktutė, sacrifices her career in the arts with the intention of becoming a countryside teacher. Stories about the romantic sacrifices of young people were the tradition of the period, and appealed to the intelligentsia. The women of the *Old Manor* are talented, reasonable, but irresolute mothers and daughters from the intelligentsia and from peasant heritage. They are extremely valuable in that they provide the reader with a comprehensive social and psychological depiction of Lithuanian upper-class women as well as country peasants in the late nineteenth century.

EARLY INDEPENDENCE

Independence lasted only a brief twenty years, and did not significantly change society nor women's status. It did, however, initiate important progress in the growth of towns, the development of education—such as the reopening of Vilnius University—and in the emergence of capitalism. Literature entered a new phase after the prohibition of the Lithuanian press was lifted in 1905. This period is marked by a number of new authors, such as I. Šeinius, A. Vienuolis-Žukauskas, V. Mickevičius-Krėvė, and V. Mykolaitis-Putinas. Their knowledge of language and literature was considerably more sophisticated than earlier Lithuanian authors.

The new constitution granted women political rights, and, most importantly, the right to vote. Women began to enter gymnasiums and to study at the University. The newly developing towns offered employment opportunities for girls as typists, nurses, and teachers, and, by the early 1930s, the first women doctors and lawyers had graduated from the University of Kaunas.

An increase in the number of women writers could have been expected during this period, but, for several reasons, this did not happen. World War II, and the long years of occupation and fighting, had reduced the number of intelligentsia. Literature demands higher education, skill, time, and the appropriate social environment. Attitudes toward women's education and their general status had to be improved before their literature could develop. Only Salomeja Nėris and I. Simonaitytė wrote successfully during this midwar period.

Salomeja Nėris (S. Bacinskaitė 1904–1945) was the most popular poetess of the midwar period in Lithuania. Her poetry was, by no means, modern in the context of European poetry, but it marked a step forward from the nineteenth century to the twentieth century in Lithuanian language and literature.

Representing the generation born under independence, Nėris came from a rich peasant family, and Lithuanian was her mother tongue. She studied at a gymnasium and at the University. Although her education had an impact on her poetry, her heart remained in the countryside. She had spent her childhood in a closed rural society, and urban life, with its harsh brutality scared her. She could not comprehend its complications and was lost in the vast array of social ideology.

The early verses of Nėris were highly subjective and emotional. She declared personal liberty in a positive and somewhat abstract manner. She wrote in her diary, "The passion of life, of a complete earthly life, was born in me. It urges me to suffer its torture and to participate in its joy." The emotions of her diary eventually became poetic verse. "I love life in a strong way, . . . that only youth is capable of."

Nėris believed that love could free her of all her problems, and liberty was her credo. Such emotional extremities were not tolerated by traditional society, and so she faced opposition and misunderstanding. Nėris offered the following definition of the woman: "The whole essence of a woman is in just a single word—love," and she explained, "I shall be a woman, not just a female. I shall be his friend, not a lover. I shall be his wings, not a stone tied to his neck."

She wrote in her diary, "Yes, I am a woman of flesh and fiery blood. But I am not just a woman, I have learned to endure, I am not scared, I can face torture, I, the 'sinner,' can face the 'saints' in a fearless manner. . . . " None of her predecessors could have used such words. Their very way of life would not have allowed them.

Years later she wrote in her diary, "Human flesh, swarms at two ends of the bridge: feminine to the right, mixed at the left, masculine still farther . . . I loath the naked pieces of flesh stretched-out in different postures. I agree with Schopenhauer, when he loathes the female body."

Whether by choice, or by absence of choice, she lost herself to the Stalinist totalitarianism. Her last verse, "On the Big Road," recounts the painful shock of betrayal by friends and political allies. The first to write so frankly, paid a high price and was eventually destroyed by politics.

EMPIRE AGAIN

After World War II, massive emigrations and postwar deportations, left Lithuania without most of its intelligentsia. A new wave of intelligentsia emerged. Innovation, which had been concentrated in towns, was, once again, dominated by people from the rural areas. Society became enslaved to the ideology of socialist realism and totalitarianism. Authors of both prose and poetry fought for survival and eventually learned ways of expression that could pass Soviet censorship.

This tenacious culture that had already survived two crises in the twentieth century was defeated by the third. Literature survived through language and a cultural determination which had developed during the nineteenth century. Language, as the main cultural feature of our nation, had helped to preserve our heritage through the work of literate people and writers many years before independence occurred.

THE NEW GENERATION OF WOMEN AUTHORS

Current women authors include V. Jasiukaitytė, J. Ivanauskaitė, and J. Skabliauskaitė. Some of their books have caused scandals and sensations, but all use new themes and modern forms of expression. Following are some short reviews of recent books to give an indication of what our modern women writers are saying.

Miraculous Grass of Fenceside by Jasiukaitytė searches for new forms. It is an approach to "magical realism" that "should be felt rather than perceived." Again, we see that the main characters and bearers of Lithuanian culture are women.

Funeral by V. Juknaitė was edited just before the restoration of independence and describes the difficult transformation process from a rural to an urban way of life. At first glance, this novel is a history of traditional rural Lithuania. Women are the vivid souls of a Lithuanian village, old and beloved, forgotten by sons and daughters, happy and unhappy. As women who witnessed the war and the postwar events, they experienced poverty, treachery and injustice. They also witness their one final loss—the death of the village itself. Their children have migrated to the towns, their husbands have gone or become alcoholics, and the women are doomed to lonely deaths. Rural to urban contrast of such strength is rare in Lithuanian literature.

In *Women of Liunasargis*, Skabliauskaitė gives us a lonely woman, the inhabitant and protector of a swamp, who is forced to live in a town which she does not wish to understand. The simple and clear logic of Liunasargiai no longer exists. Drastic changes occur as she becomes enslaved by a new comfortable life. She is a stranger in town and a stranger to herself. Her life had been simple and clear, and the relationships were equally simple and direct. Now, priorities, manners, and solutions seem to be distorted by the town as in a curved mirror.

The Witch and the Rain by Ivanauskaitė provoked screams from bigots, and heavy sighs from moralists. The book was banned by the church, and it was scrutinized for pornography, but none was found. In it, Ivanauskaitė attempts to break several social taboos. The book includes love with a Catholic priest and several descriptions of physical and moral "striptease." Until this time, even descriptions of normal sexual intercourse had been avoided by even the boldest male writers. Despite its sexual content, it was the plot, by taking liberties with the life of Christ, that caused the real scandal. Ivanauskaitė describes three pairs of characters: Marija of Magdal, the great sinner and the loyal follower of Jesus Christ; Maria Victoria, the lover of St. Paul of Birds; and modern Victoria, who is in love with Paulius, a monk and a priest.

Ivanauskaitė seems to say that only women are capable of real love, whereas a man's love is incomplete. Her female characters are convincing and interesting. Each of them is the incarnation of a single emotion, and each in her own way suffers from an insufficiency of love. Marija Magdalena, overwhelmed with self-renunciation, finds spiritual love in her appreciation for being forgiven her sins. Maria Victoria is doomed to a limbo of physical and spiritual love, and Victoria finds no release in her physical love and seeks the help of a psychoanalyst.

The three women are one body but three souls. They introduce distortions and entanglements that are intensely difficult—namely, jealousy, altruism, loyalty, and treachery. The modern Victoria comes to the conclusion that the world of passion is "the road to hell." Far from lost, she is the rational urban soul, as well as the product of education and a new culture. The novel, with its layers of everyday life, is a romance of modern urban life. It clearly illustrates the evolution of both literature and of Lithuanian women writers progressing from everyday documentalists to writers and thinkers tackling problematic issues on a world scale.

CONCLUSION

Throughout the twentieth century, the influence of the rural intelligentsia has been an important factor in retaining Lithuanian language and culture. This is true, not only because most of our authors were of rural origin, but also because the feudal agrarian model was never replaced by capitalist solutions. Because of the survival of deep Lithuanian beliefs, which were developed through centuries of history and mythology, the ideas of sacred earth and work remain rooted in the plots and in the life-attitudes of our literature.

The recent literature by women is complicated, multilayered and highly perfected in an artistic sense. The progress by women authors is illustrated by comparing the early works by Žemaitė, Šatrijos Ragana, and Salomeja Nėris with the more complex and developed works of modern female authors. The new authors describe the immense changes in our society and how they are affecting women, thus creating an important transition in our literature.

Women authors in Lithuania—such as Salomeja Nėris, V. Juknaitė, V. Jasiukaitytė and J. Ivanauskaitė—revealed to us the agonies of rural culture and demonstrated the internal conflicts and difficult transitions to urban life. The present generation of women writers explore the fate of uprooted individuals living in urban society.

REFERENCES

Ivanauskaitė, J.
1993. _Laume ir lietus (The Witch and the Rain)_. Vilnius.

Jasiukaitytė, V.
1981. _Stebuklinga patvorių žole. (Miraculous Grass of Fenceside)_. Vilnius.

Juknaitė, V.
1988. _Sermenys. (Funeral)_, Vilnius.

Lowmianski, H.
1949. _Z zagadnien spornych spoleczenstva litewskiego w wiekach srednich_. Przeglad Historyczny. T.XL.

Nėris, Salomeja
1990. _Works_. Vol. 1–3. Vilnius.

Ragana, Šatrijos
1964. _Selected stories_. Vol. 1–2. Vilnius.

Skablauskaitė, J.
1993. _Liunasargių moteris (Women of Liunasargis)_. Vilnius.

Žemaitė
1956. _Selected works_. Vol. 1–6. 1952–1956, Vilnius.

Chapter 3

Life Histories: Three Generations of Lithuanian Women

Agnė Pankūnienė

GRANDMOTHER

My grandmother was born in 1922 in the village of Verbališkės, which is eight kilometers outside of Kaunas. Grandmother was the tenth and last child in her family, her oldest sibling being eighteen years her senior. She came from a family of prosperous farmers, the landed gentry. They owned ten hectares of land and usually employed two workers to help on the farm. Her father was hardworking and loved his land.

When Grandmother was three years old, lightning hit her family's house and cattle shed. It burnt the house down and killed almost all the cattle. It was a tragic misfortune for them, but the land was fertile, and her father worked very hard to overcome the setback. Step by step, he rebuilt the home and the farm.

At the age of seven, Grandmother began attending primary school. She went to school for six years and completed primary school, but she did not continue on to high school for two reasons. First, she was anemic and suffered from weakness. Second, after the fire, the financial state of her family was not good. The family could not afford to send her to school. Instead, they paid for her elder brothers to finish primary school and high school, and they went on to learn a trade. She says that's how it was back then. The education of girls came second.

Grandmother wanted to become a nurse. Six months after she finished primary school at the age of 14, she went to live with her uncle, an eminent eye doctor in Šiauliai. She worked as his assistant, but his health was failing, and, after two years, she returned home to her parents.

In 1941, at the age of nineteen, Grandmother married a man who was twelve years her senior. She went to live with her husband and his parents in the village of Gaižėnai, three kilometers from her own village. His parents were also farmers who owned five hectares of land, and needed their son's help with the farm.

In 1943, Grandmother bore a son. While her husband worked on the farm, she looked after their son and helped her mother-in-law with domestic chores. Two years later, Grandmother had a second child, a daughter. Her husband was an electrician, and got a job in the city of Kaunas where the family moved and rented a flat. That same year, her father-in-law died.

After the Soviet takeover, Grandmother's husband was deported to Siberia. When he was young, he had belonged to *Jaunalietuviai* (Young Lithuanians), a Lithuanian youth organization. Later, he had become a member of a national political organization *Šauliai*. Those were his crimes, and, for them, he was sentenced to fifteen years in Siberia. When his mother found out about his deportation and the length of his exile, she went mad with grief. Grandmother had to leave Kaunas and return to Gaižėnai to take care of her mother-in-law.

Grandmother says that only her faith in God helped her to survive those years. Her husband was gone. Her mother-in-law was mad. She had two small children to care for, with no steady job, and the Soviets appropriated most of the farm. She would travel to Kaunas and work doing menial jobs, such as cleaning houses and doing other people's laundry. In the evening, she worked on the farm where she bred cows, pigs, hens, and cocks.

In 1951, her mother-in-law died, and, in the next year, the barn burned down. So, Grandmother sold what was left of the farm, and she and the children moved back to Kaunas. She rented a flat and worked part-time doing whatever she could to support her family. After two years, she finally got full-time work chopping and sorting meat in a meat-packing factory. As a state employee, she was entitled to a small plot of land on which to build a house. She immediately built a lean-to, and she and the children lived there for a few years.

In 1956, after ten years in Siberia, Grandmother's husband returned to Kaunas. His years in Siberia, and living under harsh

Soviet conditions, had ruined his health, and he often had heart pains. Despite this, he found a job as an electrician. Five years later, they built a house near the meat packing factory. It was a big house with two stories and a good cellar. However, the stability of a home and a husband did not last long. In 1966, Grandmother's husband died of a heart attack.

After working in the meat packing factory for twenty-two years, and at the age of fifty-three, Grandmother went to work in a shop as a salesperson. The work was easier, so she was not as tired at the end of the day. Three years later, with her children grown and gone, she sold her house and bought a small one room flat in the center of Kaunas. The following year, she retired on her pension.

In 1983, her son died. She says that, of all her trials and tribulations, this one was the worst, and the most painful event in her life. Her son was her favorite child. They were very close, and he was always good to her. He was unhappy in his personal life, and the events which led to his death were never determined. He was found frozen to death near the Kaunas Sea. For a year following his death, Grandmother was despondent and could not overcome her sorrow.

After this tragedy, Grandmother moved again—this time to be near her daughter and grandchildren. She now lives in a two room flat with her grandson, my brother. She has worked hard all her life, but is still strong and full of vitality. She comes to our home almost every day and cooks dinner. At the age of seventy-three, she works on our family farm plot, planting and weeding. I never hear her say that she is tired. In fact, she outlasts my mother and me.

She has suffered a great deal, but all she asks from life is for her daughter and grandchildren to have a better and easier life than her own. Not long ago she told me, "All my life, I served other people, but I don't want others to have to serve me. I pray to God for a quick and easy death."

MOTHER

My mother was born in 1945 in the outskirts of Kaunas. She was the younger of two children. Her brother was three years older. She was only one year old when her father was deported to Siberia. She spent her early childhood in the village of Gaižėniai with her mother, her brother and her paternal grandmother. She was the favorite niece of one of her maternal aunts who often invited her to come and stay with her. The aunt was rather rich and bought her shoes, dolls, and sweets. Despite the welcomed luxury items, my mother did not want to live with her aunt. She preferred to live in poverty with her own mother.

After her grandmother had died and the barn had burnt down, her family moved to Kaunas. When Mother was eight years old, she began to attend school. She was a good student and liked to participate in extra activities. She danced, sang in the choir, and played volleyball.

When she was eleven, her father returned from Siberia, but he never regained his health. Times were difficult in the city for her family. Butter, sugar, and flour were sold only for Soviet holidays. You had to wait in very long lines for basic goods, which were rationed, and, after the long wait, you could buy only one kilogram of the desired products.

At the age of fifteen, Mother became a member of the *Komsomo* (Young Communist League). It was very difficult to enter university or other training institutes without being a member of this league. She excelled in the league and was elected secretary.

In 1964, Mother graduated from secondary school and was admitted to the Chemical Technology Faculty at Kaunas University of Technology. A popular specialization during this period was artificial fiber chemistry, and Mother decided to pursue studies in this area. However, the faculty officials decided that the country had enough fiber specialists and instructed her to choose another subject. She applied for a specialization in food product technology. There was competition for this specialization, but Mother was an excellent student, and, after completing one year of study, she returned from her summer holiday to find that she had been chosen to study public catering, organization, and technology. She conducted butter research, took part in conferences, and wrote scientific articles. She was also active in the Student Scientific Association.

Mother was twenty-one when her father died. Three years later, during her final year at the university, she married. Mother met my father at a disco, and they dated for three years before they married. He was also in his final year at Kaunas University of Technology, with a specialization in automatics. Father was from a small town, Telšiai, which is about two hundred kilometers from Kaunas. After they married, they lived with Grandmother in her house. My mother's brother was married one year before my mother, and he lived with his wife's parents.

In the spring of 1970, Mother was offered a position at the university, but the salary for young lecturers without advanced degrees was very low, and she was pregnant. So, she turned the job down. Her husband, an excellent student, was also offered a job at the university. He decided to accept the offer and continue his education. Male students were exempt from the Soviet army, and this influenced his decision to stay at the university.

Mother was at the top of her class and was able to secure a good job despite a lot of competition. She received a position as a technologist at Unification Baltija. This organization managed several cafes and restaurants in Kaunas. One restaurant, Baltija, which is in the center of town was newly built and was located in one of the most prestigious hotels in Kaunas. She enjoyed her work which included creating new recipes and expanding the assortment of desserts. She also arranged exhibitions on cookery and confectionery.

Mother was pregnant when she started working, and, after four months on the job, she bore a son. She stayed home for three months after my brother's birth. At that time, three months was all the maternity leave that was granted. When she returned to work, my brother was placed in a state nursery for day care. I was born in 1973, and, again, Mother stayed home for three months, and then, once again, entrusted her children to the care of the state.

After one year on the job, Mother was promoted to assistant director of the Baltija. She was responsible for food ordering, nutrition, and service. The hotel entertained high-level government officials and had to be well-run. She did her job well, and, in 1976, she was elected chairwoman of the Restaurant and Cafe Trust Trade Union. She stayed in that position for five years, assuming responsibilities of work environment conditions, maintenance of housing, and managing the affairs and cultural lives of the workers. One of the attractions of the new job was a new flat. Grandmother sold her flat and came to live with us. Both women worked, and my brother and I continued being cared for by the state. Mother would pick us up from the nursery laden with big shopping bags, take us home, cook dinner, and help my brother with his homework. After we went to bed, Mother would knit. This was her favorite hobby, knitting while watching TV.

In 1980, I began primary school. My grandmother retired and took over the shopping, the cooking, and the washing. Everyone became a little happier and more relaxed. My brother and I loved having Grandmother at home.

In 1981, my mother returned to her previous job as assistant director of the Baltija. She was responsible for the reconstruction of the restaurant Metropolis, which had been a landmark restaurant on Kaunas' pedestrian promenade. She managed the renovation of the restaurant right down to the table cloths and dishes. In 1985, Metropolis finally reopened, and my mother was made the manager. In 1986, she was transferred and appointed to a position as director of another restaurant collective, *Unification Kastytis*. This collective was composed of restaurants and cafes in the old-town district of Kaunas. While this was considered to be a promotion, it upset my mother to leave Metropolis. She had grown very attached to the restaurant while making all the plans for its reopening.

In 1990, when Lithuania regained its independence, all of the restaurant collectives were divided into smaller enterprises. The entire Kastytis Unification was reduced to only one restaurant, The Kastytis. Mother went from being director of several restaurants to managing only one. To make matters worse, in 1992, Kastytis was privatized and became a joint stock company. Mother was elected Director and given 10 percent of the stock. However, the financial potential of the restaurant today is not good. Located far from the center of town, it is outdated, and needs investment to attract a new clientele. Poor people cannot afford to go out to dinner, and the rich want to go to fancier places. The Kastytis functions mainly as a funeral-dinner restaurant, where families give dinners after burials. The bar does some business, and the kitchen sells its confectioneries to local supermarkets.

During the Soviet period, things were better for my mother. She had a good job and a good salary. When she was the chairperson of the Restaurant and Cafe Trust Trade Union, almost every year she went on a trip to other Socialist countries, such as Poland, Czechoslovakia, and Hungary. Now, her greatest diversion—although it is also a lot of hard work—is our collective garden.

Every summer, our family used to go on holiday to Palanga on the Baltic Sea coast, but we cannot afford to go anymore. Mother's paycheck is spent on food, and nothing much is left after that, and my father pays for the utilities with his money. For the last two years, Mother has taken only one, one-week vacation, even though she was entitled to a month.

Mother has only only seven more years until she can retire on her pension, but pensions these days are not enough to live on, and she is very uncertain about her future. As long as the restaurant stays open, she will work there—unless of course, she is offered a better position elsewhere.

AGNĖ

When I was born in Kaunas in 1973, my parents and brother lived with my maternal grandmother. My father was a lecturer at the university at this time, working very hard to prepare his thesis to become an associate professor. Mother was working as an assistant director of a restaurant collective. She stayed home with me for three months, and then returned to work, after which I was cared for in the state nursery.

When I was two years old, I began preschool. I hated going, but there was no one to look after me at home, and my mother had no choice. In 1978, she received an allocation from her job to buy a four-room flat. During the Soviet period, there was a shortage of housing, and, in order to get a flat, you had to have an assignment from your working place. Some people had to wait as long as ten years. We were lucky and happily moved into our new home. I then went to a new kindergarten which was nearby. An unpleasant memory I have from childhood concerns all the other children in kindergarten being picked up by their mothers, and my mother not being there. I was picked up by a neighbor who also had a child at the kindergarten. My mother was always very busy, and returned home from work late, tired, and nervous. She didn't want to listen to my brother's and my problems. She simply wanted rest. All my joys and problems were discussed with friends, because I felt that my mother did not have time for me.

In 1980, I started primary school. That same year, my grandmother retired and was able to spend a lot of time at our flat. It was nice for my brother and me to come home to a good dinner cooked by Grandmother. It made things easier for Mother too. She no longer had to do all the shopping, cooking and cleaning.

In primary school, I did not excel or even get good grades. That changed in fifth form, when I became friends with a girl who was a very good student. I do not really understand why, but my studies improved. Maybe I was ashamed of my poor grades and wanted to have the same high grades as my new friend. So, in the sixth form, I earned all fives (the highest grade), and, by the time I finished secondary school, I had a 4.9 grade point average.

In 1991, I finished secondary school and entered Kaunas University of Technology. I decided that it would be the best place for me to learn the skills I would need for a successful career. It is geared toward women, and it has a good reputation for placing students in well-paid jobs. After my second year there, I assisted in the admissions department, working alongside the Dean. After our admissions work was completed, she offered me a job in the United Arab Emirates, working for two months as a secretary. I immediately agreed to go. It turned out to be good preparation for me. I improved my English, and I learned how to use fax and telex machines. It was like a vacation and a job at the same time. I worked in the mornings and the evenings, but had my afternoons to myself. I spent my free time on the beach of the Persian Gulf. It was an interesting and wealthy country. My room in the hotel included maid service which was quite a luxury for me. But it was still strange not to see trolley buses jammed with people.

In September, I returned to Lithuania and my studies. The following summer, I married a young man, also a student whom I had met two years earlier in a disco. He is working on a master's degree in electronics and is also taking management courses.

That October, I began a secretarial job that I had gotten through a friend who worked at the same firm. This is the easiest way to get a job, although it is also possible to find work through recruitment at the faculty. The job was OK, because I had free time and could coordinate my studies with my work. On the other hand, the firm didn't really need a secretary. There was not enough work to keep me busy, so I made coffee and did other menial tasks. After six months, I quit. I was bored and did not feel useful. Two months later, I began to work as a secretary in another firm. I like this firm much more than the first one because I am given responsibility and am learning new things. My husband also began working as a electronics salesman in a small department store.

My future is uncertain. I have just graduated from Kaunas University. I don't want to spend my life doing secretarial work. Secretaries have to take orders from their bosses, and I want to do something more independent, perhaps work in marketing.

I believe that I have two main opportunities. First, I could work and continue my studies, getting an advanced degree. Or second, I could—and would like to—return to the United Arab Emirates where my husband and I could live independently. We currently live with my parents and have to share their car. We would also be financially independent, whereas now, we rely on my parents for help. Because we are both working, this dependence should change, but not substantially. If you work honestly—meaning outside of the Lithuanian Mafia—it is very difficult these days to save enough money for your own flat or car.

What about my plans for the future? At the moment, I am not ready to have a family. My husband wants children now, but I prefer to wait until our future is more certain. I would also like to reach certain career and financial levels before I have children. This is important for my future and for theirs.

Chapter 4

Women in the Domestic Domain

Giedrė Purvaneckienė

INTRODUCTION

It is widely accepted that family is the most important realm of Lithuanian women's lives. This is true, but what does family mean to them? Why it is so important? Do Lithuanian women differ from other women in the world in their attitudes toward family? What historical conditions formed contemporary values, attitudes, and views? Why does Lithuanian society assign to women a primary role in the family and a marginal role in society?

HISTORICAL PERSPECTIVE

According to historians and ethnographers, Baltic tribes were basically egalitarian. It has been suggested that the region was matrilinear in the prehistoric era. Based on studies of Baltic mythology, Marija Gimbutas concluded that there "... are quite eloquent testimonies to a gynocentric religion supervised by women and of a matrilinear structure of society." (Gimbutas 1985, 24).

In the first Lithuanian state—The Grand Duchy of Lithuania, established in 1236—all men were warriors. In contrast to other Western European states, peasants were trained to ride horses and to participate in war campaigns (Karciauskienė 1983). Many Lithuanian historians proclaim this with pride, maintaining that this strategy enabled our small nation to conquer an immense territory spanning from the Baltic to the Black Sea. I state these historical facts not to praise our brave Lithuanian warriors, but rather to examine the effects of these conquests from a different point of view.

Who was responsible for the economy during these war campaigns? Who was responsible for the family? The Lithuanian historians are silent about this. The prolonged absence of men implies that women played a significant role in the economy as well as in the family. The first written law—the First Statute of the Grand Duchy of Lithuania, written in 1529—contained a chapter on the gentry women's property rights. This was unique in medieval Europe, and it granted Lithuanian women more rights than women in neighboring states. Kavolis (1992) states that this First Lithuanian Statute liberated women. In my opinion, and to the contrary, written law was influenced by customary law, and legal confirmation of women's rights reflected norms in society. However, regardless of its origin, this statute does prove that Lithuanian women—at least those of the gentry—had some degree of economic independence.

Later influences from the West and East, as well as from the Catholic Church, gradually weakened the position of Lithuanian women. During the first period of Russian rule, 1795–1918, Lithuanian women lost their property rights (Lithuanian Encyclopedia 1959). Despite this loss of legal rights, the Russian oppression also inadvertently created a role for them which raised their status.

After a revolt in 1863, the Russians banned Lithuanian literacy and the Lithuanian press. Loss of exposure to the Lithuanian language left a cultural void which women stepped in to fill. During this period, there were widespread underground schools, many of which were run by women. Girls were taught almost on an equal basis with boys. In fact, girls often received more attention as their teachers prepared them to be future teachers for their own children. Thus, in the times of the Lithuanian literacy prohibition, women played a special role as educators for their families and for society as a whole. This is supported by historical records. During this period Lithuanian girls had the lowest attendance of state schools in the entire Russian Empire. The General Census of the Russian Empire in 1897 proves that the majority of women in Kaunas Province were literate in a non-state language (Karciauskienė 1983).

After the proclamation of Lithuanian independence in 1918, historical records confirm the involvement of women in public life. In 1920, Lithuanian women participated in elections to the *Seimas* (parliament), and ten women were elected as delegates. The Provisional Constitution, adopted in that same year, established equal rights for men and women. Women parliament members representing the Christian Democratic Party succeeded in having an amendment adopted in 1922 which restored women's property rights (Lithuanian Encyclopedia 1959). In the early 1900s, Lithuanian women had at least as many legal rights as did women in Western Europe and the United States of America, and, in some cases, more.

What about family laws? These were directly influenced by the Catholic Church, and legal marriage was performed in the Church in accordance with Church law. Women did not lose their property rights when they married. They could own and manage their property separately. Yet, a distinction was made between the duties of husbands and wives (Civil Code 1933). A husband's duty was to provide for his wife according to his capabilities. In contrast, a wife's duties were to be obedient to her husband as the head of a family, to love him, to try to please him, and to be a devoted housewife. The law also proclaimed that a husband and wife had to co-reside, and, when a husband relocated, his wife had to accompany him.

It is widely believed that in Lithuania, during the period between World Wars I and II, the most prevalent family model was structured with the husband as provider and head of the family, and the wife as homemaker. To get a more concise picture concerning women's activities during this period, we asked one thousand Lithuanians if their mothers worked when they were between the ages of one to fourteen (Purvaneckienė 1994a).[1] The respondents, who are now older than sixty, were born prior to 1934, so their answers should reflect the situation in prewar Lithuania. Their responses indicate that 44 percent of the women worked outside the home despite the fact that they had children younger than fourteen years of age. Moreover, our question pertained only to paid labor. Thus, respondents did not include labor on their own farms. In 1939, 77 percent of Lithuanians lived in rural areas, and many of them owned farms (Department of Statistics 1993). On those farms women performed unpaid agricultural labor. There was a clear sexual division of labor within the family, but women's work was not limited to the domestic domain.

Based on these facts, we can conclude that, in prewar Lithuania, the majority of women were engaged in paid labor or working on their family farms. The assumed "traditional" family model—with man as provider, woman as homemaker—was never predominate in Lithuania. The traditional Lithuanian family is a myth—one that is widely believed, and sets up an ideal which encourages women to devote themselves to family life.

LITHUANIAN WOMEN AND THE SOVIET REGIME

During the Soviet period equal rights were legally guaranteed in society and in the family, but unfortunately, equal legal rights did not translate into equality. In short, the situation of women can be characterized in the following way: the majority of women worked fulltime and had the lion's share of domestic responsibilities. The result was the classic double, or even triple, burden. There was no choice for women to work or not to work. Every citizen was obligated to work by law. State child-care facilities were available to everyone. It seemed that the state, by involving women in the workforce and providing day care, had liberated women from dependency on men, thus striking a blow to patriarchy. The difference between patriarchy in capitalist and socialist countries is that women experienced private patriarchy in capitalism and public patriarchy in socialism (Ferree 1995). Under socialism, the state, as patriarch, had a direct relationship with women, both as mothers and workers.

The concept of state as patriarch, however, varies to some extent in Lithuania as compared to other Socialist countries because of Lithuanians' strong family orientation (Purvaneckienė 1993). There were several reasons for the heightened importance of the Lithuanian family.

First, the family was the political and national unit of opposition to the state which Lithuanians deemed to be alien and hostile. Second, the importance of the family was reinforced by the Catholic Church. Finally, economic conditions kept families together and supportive. In Lithuania, subsidies for child care and other basic necessities were not as high as in other Eastern European nations, and the difference in living standards between one-income and two-income families was significant. Drastic housing shortages made divorces and separations difficult. Thus, families were important for cultural, religious, and economic reasons.

Instead of discussing public patriarchy in Soviet Lithuania, we can speak about dual (public and private) patriarchy. Lithuanian women endured both. Private patriarchy and male dominance were weakened by state, but never eliminated. The state provided jobs, but work was obligatory. The state also provided child-care facilities, but women were not allowed to decide for how long they would take care of their children at home. The Soviet state did not provide women with equality in the workplace nor in the family. This lack of freedom of choice was another form of state intervention which attempted to define the role of women. It was patriarchy disguised as equality.

During the final years of the Soviet regime, shortages of food and other goods created new work for women—namely, waiting in queues. Despite technological progress, women became even more burdened. In 1990, a time/budget survey of workers found that working women spent an average of four hours per day performing household chores. At the same time, men spent 1.4 hours per day on household chores (Department of Statistics, 1992). Ironically, full equality was declared everywhere. Living behind the Iron Curtain with propaganda and the dominant Soviet ideology made many people believe that real equality had been achieved. They could not imagine that equality of a different nature—one based on partnership—could even exist. Therefore, it is understandable that the majority of women now reject ideas of equality which they equate with the "equality" they experienced under the Soviet regime.

After the restoration of independence, the slogan "Return Women to the Family" became extremely popular and influenced the majority of men as well as women. To men this slogan carried an implied message: the restoration of their patriarchal power. On the other hand, women were so burdened and so wearied of compulsory treatment by the state, that they did not heed the danger in this slogan. In fact, many women were eager to give up the double burden of being overworked both in low status jobs and at home. Not surprisingly, almost no one thought about returning men to the family.

In general, women's situations, as compared to the Soviet period has not improved. In fact, it has declined because of our current economic problems. From 1990 to 1993, while almost half of the day-care centers were closing, it was also becoming clear that women still needed to work because the majority of families could not survive on one salary (Department of Statistics, 1994). Currently, women do not have the luxury of deciding whether to work or not to work. Instead, they must solve the problem of finding a job. One set of problems were exchanged for another. No one can deny that society moved toward democracy. The shift in the political freedom is undeniable. But how did it affect the status of women? Are democratic changes reflected in family life?

WOMEN'S ROLES IN THE FAMILY

In order to research gender roles within the Lithuanian family, one thousand people older than fifteen years of age were given a series of statements relating to familial roles and asked whether they agreed or disagreed with the statements (Purvaneckienė 1994a). I found that Lithuanian views on the family have remained traditional, as 71 percent of the respondents agreed that a "man's job is to earn money" and a "woman's job is to look after the home and family." In addition, 72 percent of the respondents (76 percent of the men, and 70 percent of the women) agreed that "it is not good if a man stays at home and cares for children, and a woman goes out to work." Reflecting the current economic problems that make it difficult for a family to survive on one income, 88 percent of the respondents agreed that women need to work to supplement the family income.

How does employment affect women's performance in the family? The majority of respondents agreed with the following statements with no significant difference between men's and women's answers:

- A preschool child is likely to suffer if his or her mother works (72 percent);
- All in all, family life suffers when the woman has a full-time job (70 percent);
- A job is all right, but most women really want a home and children (83 percent); and
- Being a housewife is just as fulfilling as outside employment (72 percent) (Purvaneckienė 1994a).

These results illustrate the prevalence of patriarchal attitudes in Lithuania, which assign gender roles based on the traditional asymmetrical model of the nuclear family. Such patriarchal ideals, however, are in direct conflict with the widely accepted statement that both men and women should contribute to the household income.

A similar survey was conducted in 1990 in Lithuania by the Sociological Laboratory at Vilnius University (Purvaneckienė 1993). The responses in 1994 were very similar to those of 1990, which suggests that independence has not altered attitudes toward gender roles in the family.

Despite the persistence of traditional gender roles, there has been a slight change in choice of family model (Purvaneckienė, 1993, 1994b).[2] In 1991, 62 percent of our respondents selected a traditional asymmetrical family model with "man as provider and woman as homemaker." In 1994, 56 percent chose a more symmetrical family model in which both the husband and wife worked, and looked after the home and children together.

Women's responses showed the most change. Men were more likely than women to choose the asymmetrical model, whereas women were more likely to choose the symmetrical model. Only the youngest group of women (15 to 19 years of age) differed from this pattern with the majority choosing the asymmetrical model.

Education was also determined to be a significant factor in choice of a family model. In 1991, women with university degrees had the highest percentage of women supporting the symmetrical model (more than 50 percent). This figure increased, in 1994, to 70 percent. Here, we also find the largest difference between men's and women's opinions. In 1994, only 51 percent of the men with university degrees supported the symmetrical family model.

With other attitudes remaining constant, this single change in Lithuanians' choice of family model does not allow us to draw any concrete conclusions. The results might be related to the fact that women have started to look at life more realistically. Families simply cannot survive on one income, and, if women must work, they would like to share domestic duties with their husbands.

WOMEN'S PARTICIPATION
IN THE LABOR MARKET

To reconcile Lithuanian women's roles as both workers and mothers, Lithuanians prescribe labor force participation based on reproductive roles. My 1994 survey found that the majority of Lithuanians agreed on a married woman's career cycle.

- Prior to childbirth a woman should work full time.
- Women with preschool children should not work outside the home.

- Once the youngest child begins school, a woman should work part time.
- After the children leave home, a woman should work full time.

Have Lithuanian families successfully adjusted women's work to family life cycles? The answer is simply "No." Lithuanians place child rearing above a woman's career, yet they expect her participation in the labor market to be based upon family life cycles. All social-demographic groups agreed with these statements. However, they also acknowledge that this goal is unrealistic. It does not correspond with real life, past or present. Most women have had full-time jobs during all cycles of their family lives. Not working or working part time during the preschool years is a recent and growing phenomena. In 1994, 41 percent of 20- 29-year-old mothers with preschool children reported that they did not work outside the home (Purvaneckienė 1994a).

CHILDREN AND HOUSEHOLD

The family has many functions, including,

- That of establishing emotional and sexual relationships between spouses;
- The procreation and raising of children;
- The conferring of name and status to family members;
- The protection and psychological support of family members, leisure, and recreational activities; and
- The exchange of goods and services.

Most Lithuanians regard all these functions as important. My respondents rated the most important family role as procreation, raising children, providing material support, and establishing emotional bonds between spouses (Purvaneckienė 1994a).

The majority of the respondents (95 percent of the women and 92 percent of the men) believe that a married couple must have at least one child. More than 50 percent of both men and women believe that you cannot be happy without children. Particular emphasis is placed upon a woman's reproductive obligation. Women are considered to be inferior if they do not bear children. Seventy-nine percent of our male respondents and 88 percent of the women felt that a woman's life can be fulfilled only by having children. The pressure to reproduce is so great that Lithuanians recognize a woman's right to give birth and raise a child on her own. Despite this social acceptance of single parenting, however, 85 percent of the men and 81 percent of the women believe that a child can develop normally only in a two-parent household. The same traditional attitudes toward the family, with these same contradictions, have not changed significantly since 1990 (Purvaneckienė 1993).

In Lithuanian households, the sexual division of labor is pronounced. Women do the cooking, the laundry, and the ironing in 75 percent of the families, and, in more than 50 percent of the families, they also do the daily shopping and wash the dishes. In the domestic domain, men have only one primary chore of repairing household equipment. Household chores are shared by both spouses in less than 20 percent of the families. Younger families (20 to 39 years of age) are more strongly represented with more than 50 percent sharing the responsibilities of taking care of the sick and elderly, and doing their daily shopping equally or together. Thus, the following conclusions can be made:

• Household duties still fall mainly on women's shoulders;
• Yet relationships between spouses in younger families are based more commonly on partnership, suggesting that family relations might be moving in that direction.

In Lithuania, child care is either the responsibility of the mother or is shared by both partners. Feeding the children is usually the responsibility of women, whereas playing involves both parents. Dressing the children, caring for them when they are ill, and helping with homework is done either by the mother or both parents. This distribution of household responsibilities, researched in 1994, is similar to the results of a 1990 time/budget survey conducted by the Lithuanian Department of Statistics. This suggests that sex-specific child-care responsibilities have not changed significantly over the last four years.

PATRIARCHAL ATTITUDES AND WOMEN'S LIVES

Lithuanian ideals and attitudes concerning the family conjure up a rosy picture of domestic life. Most Lithuanians (94 percent) believe that it is important to have a fulfilling and happy family life. Seventy-eight percent of the men and 86 percent of the women stated that a successful family life is the most important thing in their lives. Sixty-six percent of our respondents stated that they would do anything to ensure that their relationships with their spouses are good, even if it means foregoing other things that are important to them (Purvaneckienė 1994b). Despite such strong sentiments about a happy family life, divorce rates in Lithuania are high, with fifty-nine divorces per one thousand marriages in 1993— and they are increasing (Department of Statistics, 1994).

Patriarchal dominance, if not a cause, is at least a factor which serves to escalate violence against women and children. Domestic violence is common in Lithuanian families. Eighteen percent of the women and 3 percent of the men reported that they had been badly beaten by their spouses. Furthermore, 13 percent of the women were battered more than once (Purvaneckienė 1994b). Domestic violence extends to the children as well, with 22 percent of the men and 16 percent of the women reporting that they had been badly beaten by their parents, and 14 percent of men and 10 percent of women experiencing battering more than once (Purvaneckienė 1994b).

CONCLUSION

Lithuanian women's lives are very complex. The domestic sphere, the family, and particularly the children are primarily their responsibilities. Women are marginalized in society, and, at the same time, the majority of them participate in the labor market. They earn less than men and are not generally participating in decision-making. They have jobs, but the traditional division of labor still exists in the household. Patriarchal attitudes predominate and reinforce a social order which prevents women from realizing their full potential. The present situation, which developed during the Soviet period, has not changed significantly since the advent of independence.

Despite the prevailing conservative views regarding gender roles and responsibilities, economic conditions do not permit Lithuanians to "return women to the family." This causes contradiction and conflict between ideals and behavior. Women suffer from these contradictions most of all. In the public sphere, they play a marginal role, and, in the domestic sphere, where patriarchal attitudes dominate, traditional gender roles result in the double burden for women. Patriarchal attitudes are the main obstacle to the democratization of our society, and they are the major factors which prevent women from realizing their human rights.

NOTES

1. Purvaneckienė 1994a, is based on Women in Lithuanian Society, a project which was financed by the United Nations Development Program. I was the project leader of this representative survey of Lithuanian men and women. The project was conducted by Baltic Surveys, Ltd., in June, 1994. One thousand women and five hundred men older than fifteen years of age were surveyed.

2. Purvaneckienė 1994b, is based on Family and Changing Sex Roles, which was financed by the Lithuanian Science and Studies Fund. I was the project leader of this representative survey of the Lithuanian population. The project was conducted by Baltic Surveys, Ltd., in October, 1994. One thousand persons older than fifteen years of age were surveyed.

REFERENCES

Civil Code
1933. *Civilinių įstatymų rinkinys.* Kaunas.

Department of Statistics
1992. *Women and Family in Lithuania.* Lithuanian Department of Statistics. Vilnius: Department of Statistics.
1993. Lithuania's Statistical Yearbook, Lithuanian Department of Statistics. Vilnius: Department of Statistics.
1994. *Lithuanian Women.* Lithuanian Department of Statistics, Vilnius.

Ferree, Myra Marx
1995. "Patriarchies and Feminists: The Two Women's Movements of Post-Unification Germany." *Social Politics.* Spring 1995.

Gimbutas, Marija
1985. "Pre-Indo-European Goddesses in Baltic Mythology." *The Mankind Quarterly,* 19–25.

Karciauskienė, Magdalena, et al.
1983. *Lietuvos pedagoginės minties bruožai.* Vilnius: Mintis.

Kavolis, Vytautas
1992. *Moterys ir vyrai lietuvių kulturoje.* Vilnius: Lietuvos Kulturos Institutas.

Lithuanian Encyclopedia
1959. *Lietuviška enciklopedija.* Nineteenth Bostonas.

Purvaneckienė, Giedrė
  1993. "Women in Changing Lithuania." In *Women Around the Baltic Sea. Part I: Estonia, Latvia, and Lithuania*, Marina Thoborg, ed. Sweden: Lund University.
  1994a. Unpublished research (see note #1).
  1994b. Unpublished research (see note #2).

Chapter 5

Lithuanian Women and Education: Discrimination and Career Choices

Palmira Jucevičienė

INTRODUCTION

How does education relate to Lithuanian women's ability to be productive citizens? Does their level of education reflect their level of activity in the labor force? Do women have equal opportunities to seek the highest levels of education? What possibilities do they have to impact the educational system as employees within the system?

In this chapter, I will try to answer these questions by analyzing data related to the status of Lithuanian women in education, and by discussing sexual equality within the Lithuanian educational system.[1]

EDUCATION IN LITHUANIA

The Lithuanian population is well-educated. More than 50 percent of the population that is fifteen years and older have completed at least secondary school (Department of Statistics 1994). At present, Lithuanian education consists of a basic education of nine years of general education, after which a student can attend high school for three years of studies, or a vocational or professional school. With such a background, students can then study at higher schools at the college or university level. Four successful years of study at a university leads to a bachelor's degree, an additional two years of specialized study leads to a master's degree, and a doctorate can be earned with an additional five years of study. Habilitated doctor is our highest degree, and it is earned by preparing a second dissertation based on the results of the Ph.D holder's self-directed research.

A close look at the Lithuanian educational system reveals general problems and sex discrimination. The more general problems—such as the lack of funding, as well as the shortage of equipment and other resources—have been caused by our current economic difficulties. The educational system receives limited financing from the national budget. Institutes of higher learning have been particularly hard hit over the last few years, and the number of university students has decreased to levels that are lower than other developed countries (Zavadskas 1994).

WOMEN IN EDUCATION

According to population census data from 1989, 18 percent of Lithuanian women had higher education, 60 percent had secondary education, and 21 percent had not finished secondary education. This can be compared with the data on men, which was 13 percent, 61 percent, and 26 percent respectively. Female students slightly outnumbered male students. Women represented 55 percent of the total number of students in 1993–1994 school year, with 50 percent of them in secondary schools, 61 percent in higher schools of college type, and 55 percent in university bachelor-degree programs. Men outnumbered women only at vocational schools, where they constituted 59 percent of the students during the 1993–1994 school year. A comparison of education levels between Lithuanian women and those of other developed countries reveals that women's participation in education at all levels is similar to or higher than countries such as Belgium, the United States of America, and Sweden (Department of Statistics 1994).

In general, more women than men have earned higher education degrees in Lithuania. In my opinion, there are two primary reasons for this phenomenon.

First, Lithuanian women are more socialized toward gaining knowledge and learning than are men. They have a historical tradition as the keepers of literacy which dates back to the ban on the

Lithuanian press. Men, on the other hand, are socialized toward work and the independence which paid employment offers.

Second, the overwhelming majority of teachers at secondary institutions are women.

However, there is a major problem in the Lithuanian educational system regarding the feminization of education. Ninety-three percent of the teachers at primary schools, and 85 percent of the teachers at secondary schools are women, even though only 36 percent of the school principals are women). Male teenagers are alienated from this female environment, and they resent being supervised by female teachers. Thus, many young men leave school after nine years of general education.

WOMEN IN HIGHER EDUCATION

The sex-ratio imbalance of students seeking higher education has created discrimination against female students. Some Lithuanian universities have quota systems which makes admission into their programs easier for men than for women. Women are not required to pass more difficult entrance exams, but they need higher scores to be admitted.

The origin of this quota system was political. Under Soviet rule, men who were enrolled in institutes of higher education were eligible for military deferments. The reluctance of Lithuanians to send their men into the Soviet army prompted many institutions to implement policies to make it easier for men to gain admission to universities, thus enabling them to avoid military service.

Despite this, women outnumber men in bachelor's degree programs. However, their numbers decrease at the master's and doctorate levels. In 1993, women represented 48 percent of the students in master's programs, 36 percent in doctoral studies, and 13 percent with habilitated doctorates (Ministry of Science and Education 1994).

To understand why fewer women pursue advanced degrees, I interviewed twenty women from three institutions—Kaunas University of Technology, the Lithuanian Institute of Physical Education, and Klaipėda University. Ten of the women were doctoral students, and 10 were master's students. They targeted the university administration as the cause of fewer women in higher education, and they claimed that the admission officials discriminate against women.

This discrimination does not end at the admissions level, it also extends to hiring practices. At the Lithuanian universities, the percentage of women lecturers with doctorates was 38 percent during the 1993–1994 academic year. Despite this, only 13 percent of the full professorships were filled by women. The breakdown of women doctoral lecturers by university was as follows:

- Vilnius University, 36 percent
- Vilnius Pedagogical University, 40 percent
- Vilnius Technical University, 11 percent
- Vytautas Magnus University, 35 percent
- Kaunas University of Technology, 52 percent
- Klaipėda University, 39 percent
- Lithuanian Musical Academy, 65 percent
- Kaunas Medical Academy, 32 percent
- Lithuanian Veterinary Academy, 22 percent
- Lithuanian Academy of Agriculture, 20 percent
- Lithuanian Institute of Physical Education, 29 percent, and
- Šiauliai Pedagogical Institute, 49 percent.

It is clear that the more prestigious jobs in the educational system are held by men. This suggests that career opportunities at the universities are better for men than for women. Such sexual discrimination could certainly discourage women from pursuing advanced degrees and from choosing academic careers.

Discussions with master's and doctoral students suggests that women have a more difficult time completing their graduate studies than do men. The reasons for this are social rather than intellectual.

Women are just as diligent in their studies, but they have more domestic responsibilities. Early marriage and childbearing means that most female graduate students already have at least one child. Lithuanian traditions dictate that mothers are responsible for child-rearing responsibilities. This takes time away from their studies. Graduate students are also faced with economic difficulties because scholarships for master's and doctoral students are too small to cover living expenses.

SEX-SPECIFIC CHOICE OF STUDIES

In Lithuania, sex-specific choice of subject to study occurs at the undergraduate and graduate levels. As in other countries, female students tend to specialize in the humanities and social sciences. Men outnumber women in technical science, mathematics, natural science, and agricultural science. In classical universities that specialize in humanities and social sciences, however, women outnumber men. For example, in 1994, at Vilnius University women constituted 74 percent of the bachelor's degree students. At Vytautas Magnus University 60 percent of those students were women, and at Klaipėda University this figure was 77 percent.

Education and premedical programs also have more women than men. The student body at Vilnius Pedagogical University is 74 percent female. At Šiauliai Pedagogical Institute, that figure is 90 percent; and at Kaunas Medical Academy, it is 65 percent. This is in contrast to Vilnius Technical University, where women constituted only 19 percent of bachelor's degree students.

CAREER GOALS

The Faculty of Administration at Kaunas University of Technology, where women prepare for business careers, is an excellent environment for researching women's careers aspirations. The faculty was established in 1990 with the goal of helping Lithuanian women to acquire quality education in business administration. It began as a faculty open only to women, but, in 1993, men were allowed to enter. The main study program—business administration—offers two degrees: a bachelor's with four years of study, and a master's with two additional years of study. These women excel both in their studies and at work. Thirty-four percent received honors, and 62 percent had good or excellent evaluations.

In 1994, 320 female juniors and seniors in the bachelor of business administration degree program were interviewed. Fifty percent of these women were already working as managers or administrators. Forty-eight percent of these students stated that they had found employment quite easily, while 30 percent had experienced some competition. The salary earned by these students equals the average wage in Lithuania, and some are earning considerably more.

Despite this, our respondents believe that sex discrimination is prevalent in Lithuania. Seventy-two percent stated that Lithuanian society favors businessmen, 40 percent have personally experienced discrimination, and 40 percent stated that the stereotype and preference for businessmen has created problems for businesswomen.

Students also perceive that men and women wishing to be successful in business need to perform differently. According to students with work experience, the characteristics of a successful businessman are ranked as follows:

1. A practical mind,
2. Logical thinking,
3. Concrete thought and actions,
4. Knowledge,
5. Ability to solve problems,
6. Ability to communicate, and
7. Ability to make decisions.

The respondents, however, ranked the characteristics necessary for a woman to succeed in business, differently:

1. Ability to communicate,
2. Good appearance,
3. Knowledge,
4. Flexibility,
5. Ability to make decisions,
6. Concrete thought and actions, and
7. A practical mind.

In 1993, I supervised a research project to examine the career plans of female students at the Faculty of Administration. One-hundred and six seniors in the business administration program at Kaunas University of Technology were interviewed.[2] The goal of the study was to investigate career aspirations, the influence of education on career opportunities, and possible career paths.

Seventy-five percent of the students stated that they planned to pursue a career, while the remaining 25 percent stated that they had no career plans. When asked about the important criteria in seeking jobs, 52 percent responded "hard work and persistence," 31 percent checked "skills and abilities," 29 percent answered "personal characteristics," 24 percent stated "knowledge," 7 percent marked "social position of their families," and 6 percent picked "financial position."

Personal efforts were considered to be more important than such factors as the social or financial positions of their families. However, the interviewees also acknowledged that success can be influenced by other factors.

In their responses to the question "What, in your opinion, are the reasons for a successful career?" 42 percent identified "favorable circumstances," 26 percent checked "personal connections," 25 percent said "hard work and persistence," and fifteen percent thought that luck or fate was important. They believe that, although one needs to work hard to progress in a career, a person's efforts might not be the main cause of success.

Most of the students stated that their career aspirations and employment goals had changed since the beginning of their studies and work experiences. Forty-four percent planned to be administrators, 37 percent wanted to be managers, 21 percent planned to be secretaries, 16 percent aimed for vice-director, and 13 percent planned to become entrepreneurs. Interestingly, 65 percent of the respondents thought that an employee's career is the affair of both employer and employee, while only 28 percent of respondents felt that this was a personal affair.

This research demonstrates that these women take their careers seriously, and that they need and desire opportunities to succeed. It is noteworthy that students emphasized education—especially their current studies at the university—as a step toward success. About half of the students planned to continue their studies and earn master's degrees.

These students also realistically evaluate women's position in society. They believe that the foundations of their careers lie in their educations. They value advanced degrees, and they have formulated solid career goals.

CONCLUSION

Reform of the Lithuanian educational system began after the reestablishment of independence, but it still has a long way to go before sexual equality in education is achieved. This is not an issue which is currently addressed. Economic and political problems are in the limelight.

Women's status in our educational system, to some extent, mirrors their status in society. Lithuanian women are comparatively well-educated, but their career opportunities are in lower status jobs, both inside and outside of the educational system. Beginning with graduate studies, the highest spheres of academe are dominated by men who also hold the top positions in the entire educational system and in the government.

We can only hope that our transition to democracy will bring about a more truly democratic society—one in which women have equal opportunities and power in Lithuania.

NOTES

1. This research is based on secondary data from various publications, and on original survey data based on my own research which involved interviews, observation, and questionnaires.

2. This research was part of a thesis project conducted by students A. Grigaitytė and I. Gusarova who were under my supervision.

REFERENCES

Department of Statistics
1994. *Lithuanian Women*. Lithuanian Department of Statistics, Vilnius: Department of Statistics.

Ministry of Science and Education
1994. Unpublished paper prepared by the Ministry of Science and Education. Vilnius.

Zavadskas K.
1994. *Vilnius Technikos Universitetas*. Vilnius.

Chapter 6

Women and the Economy

Vida Kanopienė

INTRODUCTION

Today, Lithuania, as are many other post-Communist countries, is undergoing rapid social, economic, and political changes.
The development of the country as a democratic state, and its
integration into the European community, are impossible without
the active and equal participation of women in all spheres of public
life. Therefore, it is crucial to understand the situation of women
in our society, and to examine the many existing contradictions
and problems. In this respect, women's status in the realm of
employment is of utmost importance. This chapter will discuss the
role of women in the national economy and their employment
situation during the transition period. The findings are based on
statistical data and sociological surveys (Department of Statistics
1995).[1] (Department of Statistics 1994, 1994a, 1994b, 1994c.)

THE SOVIET LEGACY

A significant and long-term trend which has had a fundamen-
tal effect on the position of Lithuanian women is their high level
of participation in the national economy. Prior to World War II,
agriculture was the most important sphere of economic activity.
About 75 percent of the total labor force was engaged in farm work

during this period (Bulletin of Lithuanian Statistics 1939). Most women worked on their family farms, combining farm work with domestic duties.

Under the Soviet regime, women were accorded an equal role in production. However, women's participation in the labor force was not a matter of choice but of obligation. The option to choose a different lifestyle did not exist. Ideologically, their economic activities were promoted as a precondition for women's liberation from domestic slavery, and, hence, sexual equality. More practically speaking, economic growth in the Soviet Union was based on the quantitative expansion of the labor force, and, thus, depended heavily on women's labor. Women's employment was stimulated by the socioeconomic policies of the state. Legislation granted women equal rights and equal opportunities in education, training, and employment. The laws and policies concerning women had two main objectives of protecting women's health, especially women who were pregnant or lactating; and improving the possibilities of combining paid work with motherhood.

The following demographic and economic factors have played, and continue to play, a significant role in women's labor force participation:

- A sex-ratio imbalance of the population was caused by World War II and subsequent Soviet deportations. The number of working-age women exceeded that of men by 75,600 in 1959, and by 36,500 in 1970. Balance in the sex ratio was reachieved only in the late 1970s (All Union 1975).
- The number of divorces was increasing. The crude divorce rate remained more or less stable (9 percent) until 1965 when it began to increase, eventually leveling off at 37 percent in 1993. This resulted in a rapid increase of one-parent families. There are more than 100,000 such families in the country today, with 110,000 children being reared by divorced mothers, and 10,000 by their divorced fathers (Department of Statistics 1994).
- Low wages made survival difficult without two incomes, and this situation persists. In fact, the living standard of the population has diminished noticeably during the years of independence. Official studies by the Lithuanian Ministry of Social Welfare showed that approximately 15 percent of the Lithuanian population lived on incomes close to the poverty line in 1989. This figure increased to 47 percent in 1991, and, in 1992, an

estimated 75 percent of the population faced poverty (Department of Statistics 1991).

• The social welfare system provided social and economic guarantees and benefits only to those participating in the national
economy. In addition, women were affected by the widespread
propaganda campaign aimed at creating a negative image of
nonworking persons as parasites who were a burden on the
community.

According to the population census data, women's general
economic activity rate increased from 66 percent in 1959 to 80
percent in 1970 (All Union 1975). The total number of women
workers increased by more than sixteen-fold during the period of
1945 to 1993, while, during this same period, men's employment
increased by only seven-fold.[2] The highest growth rate of women's
participation in the labor force was observed between 1960 and
1970. This period corresponds with the Soviet campaign towards
industrialization.

Establishing preschool child-care centers was an important
precondition for women's mass engagement in the labor force. In
1958, only 5 percent of children younger than six years of age
attended nurseries and kindergartens (Central Statistical Department 1975). Working mothers depended heavily on their own
mothers to assume child care responsibilities. However, in 1959,
when the Soviet Union began its push toward industrialization,
this picture changed.

Massive urbanization and small living quarters began to dis-
mantle the extended family, and the use of day-care centers increased dramatically. In 1985, 62 percent of all preschool children
went to state-run day-care centers. Recently, because of closures
and privatization, the number of children in day-care centers has
been decreasing and seems to have leveled off at 21 percent. Almost all rural kindergartens are closed, and the situation has wors-
ened in urban districts as well. The number of children in
kindergartens declined by more than half in 1993 (Department of
Statistics 1994).

For the last twenty years, women have comprised nearly half
of the total labor force. According to data from 1989 and 1994, 81
percent of women and 86 percent of men were gainfully employed.
This figure has been fairly constant and demonstrates that women's
prevalence rate of participation in the economy has not differed
much from that of men's (Department of Statistics 1993).

Education was a high priority for the Soviet Union. Secondary education was compulsory, and higher education was considered to be prestigious. Statistical data reveals that women students have comprised at least 50 percent of the higher school populace since 1970, and the rate of growth of women graduates exceeds that of men graduates (Department of Statistics 1991). A comparison of the education levels of economically active men and women reveals that a larger percentage of employed women have higher education. Twenty-one percent of the women and 15 percent of the men have university or higher school degrees. The percentage with specialized secondary education is correspondingly 32 percent and 20 percent (Department of Statistics 1991). It is noteworthy that, 30 years ago, these differences were less dramatic. In 1959, only 13 percent of the economically active women had higher or secondary education. The majority had not finished primary or secondary school (Department of Statistics 1994). At present, women with only a primary education constitute less than 4 percent of working women (Department of Statistics 1993).

According to the Lithuanian Population Questionnaire of 1988, only 14 percent of women with higher education, and 37 percent with only primary or uncompleted secondary education, favored the idea that "women should take care of their families rather than work professionally." Lithuanian women value their careers, not only for monetary reasons, but also for self-esteem, personal development, and contact opportunities. Our respondents felt that satisfaction with work is related, not only to occupation, but also to relations with their co-workers and a friendly working environment (Kanopienė 1992).

THE STRUCTURE OF FEMALE EMPLOYMENT

Despite high levels of education and workforce participation, the influx of women into the labor market has had little impact on sex segregation at work. In Lithuania, as in many Western European countries, men's and women's work are traditionally segregated according to sex. Women usually work in caring and service occupations or related sectors, whereas men are employed in jobs related to heavy industry, construction, and transportation. The prevalence of women in certain occupations—such as secretaries, nurses, bookkeepers, and salespeople—and the total feminization of some branches of employment—such as education, health care, the retail trade, and light industry—is characteristic of the loose Lithuanian labor force (Department of Statistics 1991). Employment in manufacturing was characteristic for the postwar generations born in the 1940s and 1950s. Recently, the social and personal services sector has gained importance, especially among young people, This sector employs more persons younger than forty years of age than does light industry (Department of Statistics 1994).

Despite the different social and economic conditions in Lithuania, as compared with developed countries, Lithuanian women followed a similar pattern of sex-specific professional specialization. In the 1980s, 46 percent of all employed women in Lithuania, 49 percent in Finland, 53 percent in Norway, 29 percent in Sweden, and 29 percent in Denmark worked at occupations in which 90 percent to 100 percent of the workers were women (Haavio-Mannila 1992). The proportion of women in male-dominated occupations in Lithuania was lower than in the Nordic countries. In Lithuania, this figure was 5 percent compared with 20 percent in Denmark, 15 percent in Finland, 14 percent in Sweden, and 9 percent in Norway (Haavio-Mannila 1992).

There are some differences in the occupation structure of women's employment in many post-Communist countries, as compared to those in the West. Lithuania has equal participation of women in some occupations which were traditionally considered to be masculine in the West. The percentage of women doctors, engineers, and architects is high. However, these professions have lower status and financial remuneration in Lithuania than in the West. During Soviet rule and the ideology of the "command economy," priority was given to the development of heavy industry and the military, while the social needs of the population were considered to be secondary or unimportant. Social-service work was not viewed as contributing to the advancement of the Soviet agenda, and, hence, it had low status. Despite the inroads made into many male-dominated professions, women still constitute the majority of the lowest level employees in these fields.

In general, women dominate the bottom of the occupational pyramid, where the lower socioeconomic job categories are concentrated. As we move up the pyramid, the proportion of women decreases, and, at the top, among the most prestigious jobs—government officials, university deans, and the like—there are very few women. According to the Population Employment Survey of 1994, the percentage of women among officials and managers is 40 percent, but the majority are concentrated in the low end of this group. Lithuanian women constitute 87 percent of the clerks, 72 percent of the service and sales workers, and 62 percent of the unskilled laborers (Statistical Yearbook of Lithuania 1995).

Sex segregation in the labor force has had the following negative consequences in Lithuania:

- It is difficult to attract men to women-dominated occupations because of a strong association that such jobs are women's work. The same holds true for women. Thus, a self-perpetuating cycle is created.
- Sex segregation promotes sex-stereotyping. Men are seen as technically-minded and object-oriented, whereas women are regarded as nurturing and people-oriented.
- Vertical sex segregation conveys the false assumptions that men are dominant by nature and should have power and leadership, whereas women are submissive and naturally willing to assume subordinate roles.

WOMEN IN THE LABOR MARKET DURING THE TRANSITION PERIOD

The situation in the labor market is rapidly changing. The introduction of the market economy has created structural changes in the labor market. Two major changes have had a great impact on women—the occurrence and growth of unemployment, and the rapid decrease of the public sector. Recent decreases in all spheres of socioeconomic development have led to reductions in employment. In 1990, the number of women in the workforce decreased by 89,000, while during this period, the number of working-age women decreased by only 9,000. Despite this, women's economic activity rates at 84 percent are higher than men's at 79 percent. This discrepancy is attributed to the unrecorded income of men's more active participation in the so-called "shadow economy," or black market and related activities (Department of Statistics 1994a).

One of the main labor-market policy programs is public service works. About twelve-thousand to thirteen-thousand people every year are involved in community service, such as building roads and other unskilled manual labor. Men fill the majority of positions offered in this program (Lithuanian Labor Exchange 1995).

Women comprise 48 percent of the workforce in the private sector or market economy, and 57 percent in the public or state-controlled sector. (Department of Statistics 1994b). The reasons for the overrepresentation of women in the public sector lies, first and foremost, in the preexisting distribution of female labor within the economy. As noted, women predominate in health care, education, and other social and personal services—the very industries which are being privatized only on a negligible scale. According to 1993 data, 222,400 of 463,000 women in the public sector are concentrated in these fields.

A different picture is observed in the private sector. Eighty-one percent of the women employed in the private sector work in manufacturing, agriculture, trade, and hotel services. (Department of Statistics 1994b).

Professions in health care, education, and scientific fields are losing their attractiveness to women for economic reasons. At the same time, activities in commerce and trade in the private sector are gaining in importance. The demand for managers, financiers, and accountants is growing rapidly, but women's opportunities in these fields are most commonly in bookkeeping, language interpreting, and secretarial work, which are the sectors of the business world with the lowest status and pay.

The increase in men's participation in the private sector—which accounts for about 60 percent of the male labor force—suggests that women are being left behind in the transition to market economy. In addition, open sex discrimination is found daily in job advertisements in the newspapers.

Most well-paid jobs offered by private firms are open only to men. A typical example is the job advertisement that was printed in *Lietuvos Rytas* (Morning in Lithuania) on 15 November 1994, which read "Worldwide foreign company is looking for sales representative. Requirements: young, dynamic, handsome male able to work with people . . . " At the same time, the most popular job offered to women is that of secretary. The usual requirements for the applicants are youth and good looks, with foreign languages and typing skills listed as a bonus.

The unwritten rule concerning sex segregation exists even in the government and related institutions. Furthermore, the structure of the Lithuanian language promotes and reinforces sex-specific job advertisements. It is not possible to advertise sex-neutral in the Lithuanian language, and the sex of the recruited person can be indicated indirectly without direct mention.

This is combined with a growing sex-based inequality concerning wages. With a rapidly deteriorating economic situation, the state is unable to pay adequate wages in the public sector. Priority is given to industry, government institutions, and the banking system. The variation in wages is increasing, and it is creating greater inequality in salaries. For example, the monthly wage in education is 32 percent lower than the average salary in the public sector, and salaries in the sciences are 29 percent lower than the public wage average. In financial professions, the salaries exceed average wages by 264 percent (Statistical Yearbook of Lithuania 1995). Thus, many previously well-paid, highly-skilled professional women find themselves close to the official poverty line.

Another important issue concerning employment is that many women, both in the private and public sector, perform strenuous manual labor under unsafe conditions. Despite official policies in the Labor Code that protect expecting and nursing mothers, regulations are being ignored. Private firms and enterprises disregard these regulations with seeming impunity. The situation is such that a special medical investigation found that morbidity rates among women workers is rapidly increasing. Women, fearing unemployment, are reluctant to stand up for their rights.

UNEMPLOYMENT

In March 1991, Lithuania adopted an Employment Law, which legally defined unemployment. Thus, unemployment registration began. The definition of unemployment includes those who are jobless, people searching for jobs, and those who have left work willingly. By the end of 1991, the number of officially registered unemployed persons was only 4,600, of which 3,000 were women. By the end of December 1994, official unemployment had soared to 33,400. Women constitute more than 60 percent of all unemployed persons (Department of Statistics 1994c).

Analysis of the unemployment trends and structure is difficult because of lack of statistical data. The official statistics give only a few indices. The data is limited to the number of women/men among unemployed/nonworking persons, and the percentage of workers. Education levels and occupation distribution are differentiated neither by demographic nor social characteristics, such as age, sex, and marital status. Very little information is available on the duration of unemployment, as well as the outcome of job searches.

In order to supplement unemployment data, I conducted research in December 1992 and December 1994 at the Vilnius Labor

Exchange, which is the state institution where the unemployed
and job seekers are registered, given unemployment benefits, and
provided with information concerning available jobs.[3] Comparison
of the 1992 and 1994 findings revealed that the proportion of women
among both the unemployed and job seekers is increasing. In 1992,
62 percent of unemployed persons and 43 percent of job seekers
were women. In 1994, these figures had risen to 79 percent and 58
percent respectively. My findings reveal that a high percentage of
unemployed women differ from other groups of nonworking persons because of their high professional and educational status. Those
with higher school or university diplomas comprise 33 percent of
the unemployed/job seekers.

Unemployed women with higher education could be divided
into four groups by branches of science: economics, engineering,
natural sciences, and humanities. Under the Soviet regime, priorities were given to engineering and technical education because of
the importance of industrialization. Women's participation in these
areas was relatively high at about 40 percent. However, during the
period of current economic reforms, and with the decline of industrial production, most of these enterprises—especially those in
mechanical, electrical, and radio engineering fields—are not working at full capacity or are closed down altogether.

These changes in the labor market translate into fewer occupations which are open to skilled women. In this respect, opportunities for women engineers, or those with diplomas in the natural
sciences, are least favorable. Women with technical educations
constitute the majority of unemployed skilled persons in Kaunas
and other industrial cities. Even in Vilnius, a city with a diversified
economy, women comprise the majority of the skilled unemployed.
Women in the humanities fare better by relying, to a certain extent, on their pedagogical skills or knowledge of foreign languages.
Women with backgrounds in economics often have additional
qualifications, such as computer skills and foreign languages, to
assist them in the new job market. According to the 1994 Employment Survey, only 25 percent of unemployed women managed to
find jobs within one to three months, while 50 percent of unemployed men found jobs in this same time period.

The opportunity to find a new job based on previous qualifications is especially important for highly-skilled professionals.
More than 80 percent of unemployed women with higher education indicated in the survey that they would prefer work which
related to their professional degrees. An analysis of the records

shows that many professional women—about 33 percent—are forced to accept jobs requiring lower qualifications or even no skills at all.

A review of labor-market policy, prepared and implemented by the Lithuanian Labor Exchange and Ministry of Social Security in 1992 to 1994, reveals that women have not been targeted as a specific group in the main objectives of the employment policy. Their policy promotes activities in the following fields:

- Labor supply and search, including jobs abroad;
- Job training and retraining;
- Support of employment for young people, the long-term unemployed, and socially disturbed persons;
- Organization of public works, such as road building and the like; and
- Assistance for small businesses.

In 1992, more than twelve-thousand people, or 10 percent of those registered at the labor exchange, were covered by these special labor-market policy programs. In 1993, this figure rose to 22 percent. Despite the rapid increase, only about 20 percent of unemployed persons can rely on the assistance of the labor exchange. The most important measures being taken are creation of new jobs, training and retraining programs, and the organization of public work. Unfortunately, there is no data on the number women covered by these policies. Therefore, their impact can be estimated only indirectly by examining the specific situation of women in the current labor market.

Women with children younger than 14 have special privileges in public-sector jobs. The employment budget is supposed to be used to create jobs for them. However, in 1994 it was reported that only 2 percent of the budget was used for this purpose in 1993, and only 1,162 new jobs were created. The length of unemployment for these mothers did not differ from other groups. Thus, this policy does not seem to be giving them any advantage in the labor market (Lithuanian Labor Exchange 1995).

When we take into account the present labor market situation and the quickly changing demand factors, it is obvious that training and retraining programs should play an important role in employment policy. However, the statistical data of the Labor Exchange reveals that only a negligible but rapidly growing number of the registered nonworking persons participate in such programs. In 1992, 1,900 took part in the program. In 1993, this figure rose

to 9,100, and, in 1994, 27,000 persons participated in the training/
retraining program (Lithuanian Labor Exchange 1995). Data on
women's involvement in this program is not available.

The retraining program has the following goals:

- Professional training of unskilled young people who are enter-
  ing the labor market,
- General training and retraining programs for adults,
- Entrepreneurship courses, and
- Retraining programs directed at the long-term unemployed and
  disabled persons

Again, none of these programs are geared specifically for women.
A review of the types of training/retraining programs offered illustrates the scant attention paid to professional women's needs. Training is offered in construction, driving, welding, metal works, carpentry,
weaving, dressmaking, and handicrafts, as well as for food-industry
workers, secretaries, word processors, and bookkeepers. In other words,
the training programs are designed within the existing economic and
occupational structure. Important factors—such as sex, age, education, and experience of unemployed persons—are not taken into con-
sideration. The opportunity to acquire modern specializations or to
gain additional qualifications is accessible to very few.

Employers prefer to hire persons who are willing to work long
hours, on weekends, and without vacations. They want healthy,
strong workers who do not have children or family responsibilities.
As job competition increases, those who are unable or unwilling to
make such commitments to their workplace will have limited
opportunities or find it difficult to enter the labor force. Women—
and especially mothers of young children and elderly women—face
serious discrimination. This situation is being virtually ignored by
policy makers and government officials. Recent laws and regulations obliging employers to pay for the first three sick days, which
were previously paid by state social insurance, will deepen sex-
specific inequality in employment because it is women who usually take time off to tend to sick children. This perpetuates a
well-established cycle. Women are discriminated against in the job
market, they accept lower paying jobs, and family responsibilities
that require absences from work are taken by mothers because the
family cannot afford loss of the father's higher income. Mothers
are, then, considered to be unreliable workers, and they experience
discrimination in the job market.

CONCLUSION

It should be stressed that, until now, neither demand factors nor the qualitative structure of nonworking persons has been adequately analyzed by government and policy makers. The issue of women's unemployment is not recognized as a pressing problem which warrants special attention.

The Lithuanian legislative and executive power is actually a "men's club" with no women representatives in the Cabinet of Ministers, and only 7 percent women deputies in the *Seimas* or parliament. It is clear that wealth and power are being concentrated in men's hands, and that they then dictate their own rules for the game. Lithuanian women might become—in fact, are becoming—one of the most disadvantaged groups in the Lithuanian labor force.

NOTES

1. I conducted research at the Employment Department in 1993 and 1994.

2. The number of divorced and widowed women aged 20 to 59 years old is more than double that of divorced and widowed men in the same age group.

3. The survey was based on sociological methods of secondary analysis using the registration cards of unemployed persons and job keep seekers.

REFERENCES

All Union
1975. All Union Census Data for 1970. Vilnius: Central Statistical Department Council of Ministers of the Lithuanian SSR.

Bulletin of Lithuanian Statistics
1939. Kaunas Department of Statistics.

Central Statistical Department
1975. *Women in Lithuania*. Vilnius: Central Statistical Department, Council of Ministers of the Lithuanian SSR.

Department of Statistics
1991. Population Census Data for 1989. Vilnius: Department of Statistics.

1993. *Women and Family*. Vilnius: Lithuanian Department of Statistics.
1994. Vilnius: Lithuanian Department of Statistics.
1994a. *Lithuanian Women*. Vilnius: Lithuanian Department of Statistics.
1994b. Labor Force and Employment. Vilnius: Lithuanian Department of Statistics.
1994c Working and Nonworking Population. Vilnius: Lithuanian Department of Statistics.

Haavio-Mannila, E., and K. Kauppinen
1992. "Women and the Welfare State in Nordic Countries." In *Women's Work and Women's Lives*, H. Kahne and J. Z. Giele, eds. Oxford: Westview Press.

Kanopienė, Vida
1992. "Family Roles of Men and Women in Lithuania." In *Norwegian Journal of Occupational Medicine*. Vol. 13:305–311.

Lithuanian Labor Exchange
1995. Labor Market in Lithuania. Unpublished internal reports of Labor Exchange 1993–1995.

Statistical Yearbook of Lithuania.
1995. Covering the year 1994. Vilnius.

Chapter 7

The Church, Nationalism, and the Reproductive Rights of Women

Dalia Gineitienė

INTRODUCTION

The ways in which society and government approach reproductive rights are a major factor affecting the status of women. In Lithuania, as in many other post-Communist countries, there is conflict over a woman's right to self-determination through control of her own body, and the agendas of the state and the Catholic Church. Women's reproductive rights are being tied to moral, legal, and social issues. Important questions concerning women's rights and the roles of women are being evaded. Instead, traditions, morals, and demographics are being discussed.

NATIONALISM AND THE STATE

Lithuania is moving toward democracy and undergoing many changes, but we must not leave half of our population behind during this transition period. Although women constitute 53 percent of the Lithuanian population, only 7 percent of the parliament is female. This male-dominated legislative body has the decision-making power over laws concerning women's reproduction. Male politicians are not asking women for their opinion. They prefer to subordinate women's rights to the interests of the state. In their platforms, many political parties address "women's problems." However, the issues discussed are family, housing, and privileges for young or large families, as if the only problems which Lithuanian women must cope with are those related to family.

Because of the recent rise in nationalism, the lack of growth of the Lithuanian population has been frequently discussed. We have a demographic dilemma in terms of decreasing birth rates and a large elderly population. Our birth rate is low—only 1.7 in 1994— which means that population is not reproducing itself (Lithuania 1993). Patriotism is invoked to promote women's reproductive role as a national interest. Slogans such as "Lithuania needs more Lithuanians," and "We are a perishing nation" have become increasingly popular in mass media and in the speeches of politicians. Motherhood is praised, and women are urged to return home to devote their lives to raising children for the motherland. However, this can only be a cause of pressure on young women who can, but do not want to, have as many children as God gives.

THE ROLE OF THE CHURCH

Prior to World War II, abortions in Lithuania were considered to be a crime, and women who had abortions could be punished with up to three years in prison (Gedvydas 1991). The influence of the Catholic Church was prominent, and having an abortion was considered as a grave sin. Women attending Catholic Church were— and still are—requested to confess the use of contraceptives. The only form of birth control accepted by the Lithuanian Catholic Church is natural family planning. Promoting natural family planning, which has an extremely high failure rate, is irresponsible. This might actually increase the number of abortions due to unplanned pregnancies.

Recently, the Catholic Church in Lithuania and the International Right to Life Organization have joined forces in a campaign to abolish the reproductive rights of Lithuanian women. Despite the popularity of the Church in the post-Communist era, the population does not necessarily agree with its current pro-life agenda. In 1994, Baltic survey data revealed that 80 percent of the respondents with higher and secondary education, 60 percent with uncompleted secondary, and 38 percent with primary education disagreed with the proposed ban on abortion.

The pro-choice voice is not heard in Lithuania. Instead there are church-sponsored conferences, seminars, and demonstrations promoting the pro-life message. In September 1994, an international conference on "Love, Family, Life" was organized by the International Right to Life Organization, supported by the Catholic Church, and hosted at Vytautas Magnus University in Kaunas. The focus of this conference was the demographic situation, natural family planning, abortion, and the psychological and moral damage of contraception. In October 1994, a conference was held at the Parliament in Vilnius titled "Lithuanian Family: Traditions and the Future." Here, problems of family, men's and women's roles in the family, demographics, and other issues were discussed by an all male panel of the Prime Minister, the Bishop, a United Nations representative, and others. In an uncontested atmosphere, our Bishop advocated, not only a ban on abortion, but on all forms of birth control other than natural family planning. Our politicians do not want to oppose the church which has reemerged as a powerful institution in the post-Communist era.

THE TRADITIONAL ROLE OF WOMEN

Another current trend is to revere role models from the period prior to the Soviet occupation—an era heralded as one of social, cultural, and economic well-being. Women are reminded to be proud of the old Lithuanian traditions of large and extended families living together in harmony. This was a time when there were supposedly no divorces, no unmarried mothers, and no unmarried couples living together. By embracing this largely fictitious portrait of the period, we mask our present problems. It does not help us to examine our current situation, nor does it find relevant contemporary solutions.

The following excerpt from a well-known short story, *"Paskenduole"* (the one who drowned herself), by Lithuanian writer A. Vienuolis, demonstrates that premarital sex and abortions were a fact of life in traditional Lithuania.

> " . . . She [Veronika] had gone to visit an old women whom she knew to be a great help to girls in "trouble." Although she had felt out of sorts for some time, Veronika could not believe she was pregnant. Today the old woman finally convinced her that she was going to have a child. Besides advice, the old women also gave her some coarse powder, for which Veronika paid ten auksinas. . . . (Vienuolis 1982).

Ultimately, Veronika's attempt at a home abortion fails, and, with no other way out, she kills herself in despair.

Those who speak about so-called "traditional Lithuanian families" are actually referring to the peasant family of the late nineteenth and early twentieth centuries. Agriculture was the main source of sustenance living for 77 percent of the Lithuanian population until as late as 1939 (Lithuania 1986). Children were valued as farm laborers and as support for aged parents. In 1945, families with three or more children accounted for 51.3 percent of the population. Infant mortality was high at 12 percent in 1939. Thus, women needed to bear more children to ensure the survival of some (Lithuania 1986).

In describing the pre-Soviet period, my grandmother asserts that large families were usually poor families. Girls as young as ten years old worked in family fields or hired themselves out to landowners for very small wages. A daughter needed a dowry, and, the larger the dowry, the greater the chances for a young girl to marry. Parents wanted their daughters to marry rich men, and, in many cases, it was the father who had the final word in deciding who his daughter would marry. The eldest son usually inherited the family farm, while the younger sons—if the family could afford it, and few could—were educated for professional life. The opportunity to acquire the skills and education for nonagricultural labor was available to few men and even fewer women.

CONTRACEPTION IN LITHUANIA

The right to safe, available, and affordable birth control, and to sex education and medical care, are crucial issues for women. The abortion issue is the most emotionally debated question concerning reproduction. Abortion is the most unpleasant, painful and dangerous form of controling fertility. However, it was, and still is, the method of birth control most commonly used in Lithuania. Soviet-made birth control pills were of such low quality that many women experienced adverse side effects, creating an aversion to oral contraceptives. Information and other forms of contraception were, and are, not widely available, affordable, or safe.

Abortions are permitted on demand until the twelfth week of pregnancy. Later abortions are allowed only with medical permission. Although the official abortion rate decreased between 1980 and 1990 from 87 to 49 per 100 live births, the number of abortions in Lithuania is still higher than in many developed countries (Lithuania 1993).

Although abortions remain legal, they are considered to be morally shameful. Many women prefer to have their private doctors perform the unregistered procedure in their own homes. They are willing to risk their health, or even their lives, to avoid public censure concerning their right to control their own reproductive systems. In addition, performing criminal abortions is a lucrative business, and unregistered procedures distort abortion data.

Current information about contraception leaves a lot to be desired. For example, one booklet explains, "If it [a condom] breaks, a women must, without delay, wash with warm boiled water, adding to one liter of water two to three spoons of vinegar" (Stankus 1982). One wide-spread belief among young women is that, when you suspect an unwanted pregnancy, you should take as hot a bath as you can endure. This is not very different from what our own grandmothers did.

There is a generally accepted myth that Lithuanians are moral, modest, and that they consider discussing sex to be shameful. Usage of words such as *sex, condom,* and *contraceptives* are almost taboo. However, according to the data of the AIDS Prevention Center, 37 percent of the five hundred students averaging seventeen years old were sexually active. Only 20 percent of the sexually active cohort used condoms (Lithuania 1993). Despite this, the former minister of education publicly stated that he did not think that the notion of "safe sex" was compatible with the program of moral education based on chastity, faithfulness, and Christian ethics being promoted in Lithuania (AIDS 1993). Young people, however, need to be taught about safe sex. When speaking about an open society, we must not forget about our rights to information, education, opinion, and self-determination.

The need for education and methods of protection against sexually transmitted infections and disease—including AIDS—is becoming critical. However, the use of all such methods depends on the cooperation of the male partner. It is common for women to get infections from their husbands, many of whom have multiple sexual partners (World Health Organization 1994). In Lithuania, 68 percent of all women afflicted with AIDS or venereal disease have had only one partner—their own husbands (Jasaitienė 1995). Men must take responsibility for the health of their partners.

THE ANTI-ABORTION MOVEMENT

Nationalists and "right-to-life" advocates argue that, because of the critical demographic situation in Lithuania, it is necessary to prohibit, not only abortion, but all forms of contraception. Nationalistic logic proclaims that a ban on abortion will increase the birth rate. Scientific data proves that bans on abortion increase illegal abortion and "abortion tourism." The World Health Organization estimates that, worldwide, five-hundred-thousand women die each year from complications related to illegal abortion (Cook 1994).

Anti-abortionists, who claim to protect the life of the unborn child, also claim that the difference between an old person and a fetus is only quantitative—that is, they differ only in the number of cells. They say that every person exists and is autonomous from the very moment of conception. Because it is not a part of the mother's body, the mother does not have the right to decide on its future. This argument can be taken a step further, as it was by Ceausescu, Romania's communist leader, who, in 1986, proclaimed the fetus to be "the socialist property of the whole society." In such case, there could be no right to physical privacy. The state would have total control over women's bodies. We have seen the human-rights violation of such state controls, as witnessed in Romania in the 1970s with their pronatalist policies, and with China until the present day with its antinatalist policies. Both countries have subjugated women's rights and health for the "benefit" of the state.

Supporters of the pro-life movement also believe that parents should prepare young people for family life. They insist that schools should not provide any information on sex education, but, culturally, Lithuanians are not accustomed to discussing these issues in their private lives. Parents are often embarrassed to tell their children even the fundamentals of sex.

WOMEN AS PRODUCERS AND REPRODUCERS

In 1955, the Soviet government legalized abortion, and social policies regarding child care and maternity issues were implemented by the state. Because women's labor was needed, these policies addressed women's role as producers and reproducers. On one hand, this allowed women the possibility of careers. On the other hand, these policies reinforced women's reproductive and child-rearing roles by granting benefits to mothers and excluding fathers.

The transition from Communism to the market economy has caused our current economic difficulties. Because of increasing economic and social insecurity about the future, having children has become a luxury. Present social benefits allow parents to raise their children at home until the child is three years old. They receive an allowance which is supposed to be linked to the rate of inflation and the minimal income level. Parents are entitled to only fifty _litas_ ($12.50) per month until the child is eighteen months old, and about twenty-five _litas_ per month until the child is three years old. Unmarried mothers receive thirty _litas_ per month until the child is sixteen years old. It is impossible to raise a child on this amount of money. Recent calculations estimate that at least three hundred _litas_ per month is needed to properly maintain one child.

Legally, maternity leave can be taken by either parent or grandparents for the whole period, or be shared between them. The tradition of women as child-rearers is so deeply rooted that it is almost always the mother who stays home with children or stays home from work when they are sick. This has many social and economic implications for women.

Because women tend to remain unemployed during the child-bearing years, they lose their professional skills during this mothering period and have a difficult time reentering the labor market. Many women in Lithuania would attest to the fact that they were dismissed from work or were not hired because they were pregnant or had a small child. Now, even our former social benefits are being eroded.

Sexual discrimination in the labor market is increasing as the state is shifting the cost of some social benefits relating to child-care sick days to private companies. There is evidence that women are being forced by their employers to sign contracts relinquishing child-rearing benefits as a prerequisite to being hired (Jasaitienė 1995).

In addition to the economic hardship of losing one's income while trying to raise children at home, the number of day-care centers has decreased by 50 percent from 1990 to 1993 (Purvaneckienė 1994). The ones that remain open are being privatized, and are, thus, unaffordable for the majority of the population. Furthermore, the use of day-care centers is considered to be unpatriotic because they are part of our Soviet legacy.

Government policies relating to women's reproductive roles should include state-paid maternity leave, with women's jobs held open for the duration, along with retraining programs, public child care, and an environment which does not diminish fertility. Without relevant retraining programs and enforcement of protective policies which do not discriminate against mothers, Lithuanian women are severely disadvantaged.

CONCLUSION

Before blaming women for the decrease in birth rates, and putting the onus on them to reverse the trend, it is necessary to improve the child-bearing environment in Lithuania. There is a need to change traditional patriarchal attitudes toward child rearing. Child care should be seen as an issue involving both parents. Furthermore, it is irresponsible to promote pronatalist policies without the necessary infrastructure and economic planning capable of handling an increased population. We need housing, day-care centers, and well-equipped schools. Unfortunately, this is not where government spending is being allocated.

Lithuanian society must become child-friendly. It must be properly prepared to accept its new members. Every child has the right to be born into a home in which it is wanted. Today, there are a large number of abandoned children. In 1993, their number rose by 54 percent from 1989. More than five hundred children younger than four years of age are institutionalized in six infant homes. Only one-third of them are real orphans. The rest are primarily from dysfunctional families who find it increasingly difficult to cope with the loss of the state-supported benefits (Lithuania 1993).

Young Lithuanian women entering our newly free and open society are facing many pressures. They have no time or energy, and no social or historical framework with which to enter the political arena and fight for their rights. In our country, they are silent. It is men and older women—neither of which can bear children—who speak the loudest. Pro-life people do not discuss women, their health, and their rights. They speak only about the rights of the fetus. Contraception protects women's health, their work-capacities, and their reproductive systems from complications of pregnancy and abortion.

With information, choices, and control of their reproductive systems, women can better control their lives. They can obtain education and employment, and they can enjoy both productive and reproductive careers. Women can also plan their child-bearing at optimal times to ensure safety for themselves, and to fortify the healthy growth and development of their children.

REFERENCES

AIDS
   1993. *Chronicle of AIDS*. Lithuanian AIDS Prevention Center. Vol. 1:8.

Cook, Rebecca J.
   1994. *Women's Health and Human Rights*. Geneva: World Health Organization.

Gedvydas, A.
   1991. "Holy right to be born." *Family*, Vol.2:22–23.

Jasaitienė, M.
   1995. "Ostrich Philosophy." *Kaunas Day*. Vol. 30:8.

Lithuania
   1986. *Lithuania: An Encyclopedic Survey*. Vilnius: Encyclopedia Publishers.
   1993. *Health and Its Problems*. National Conference on Health Policy, 29 to 30 March 1993. Vilnius.

Purvaneckienė, Giedrė
   1994. "Women in the Republic of Lithuania." *Women's World*, newsletter of the Lithuanian preparatory committee of the IV World Conference on Women. Vilnius.

Stankus, J.
   1982. "Damage of Abortion." *Republican Home of Sanitary Education*. Vilnius: Mokslas Publishers.

Vienuolis, A.
   1982. "Paskenduole: A Short-Story." Vilnius: Vaga Publishers.

World Health Organization
   1994. *Challenges in Reproductive Health Research*. Biennial report 1992–1993. Geneva: World Health Organization.

Chapter 8

Why and How the Party of Women Was Formed in Lithuania

Dalia Teišerskytė

To begin, I would like to cite the words of some well-known, lesser-known, and unknown Lithuanian people. Their words will help to emphasize the fact that it is necessary to do something real for the welfare of all the women living in our country.

———————

Historian Danutė Vailionytė: "Since women form the greater part of our society (53 percent), the health of the entire society depends upon their moral and mental well-being. I feel that our society is hostile toward women. First, we have no conception of "woman." What is the ideal woman of our times? Images are usually formed by philosophical ideology and the press. Magazines for women published before World War II focused on the image of woman as the mother who gives life to the world and possesses an enlightened personality. Look at women's magazines today. They give the impression that the ideal woman is silly and impudent. Nothing is said about a woman's intellect. The focus is on the erotic, sex, and sexist nonsense. It seems as if a woman's purpose is only to satisfy the desires of men."

Professor Dalia Brazauskienė: "The roles of women in society have changed very much. I am interested in the historical research of Marija Gimbutas which supports the idea that the role of women was particularly important in the neolith period in Europe when society was more peaceful. I think it is clear that our society is now hostile toward women. Look at women's situations in establishments of higher education. At most universities, young women outnumber men, even as students of the engineering sciences. Women are active and gifted, and they have the potential to take a more prominent place in our society. Men and women are like the two wings of a bird. If one of the two is broken, the bird cannot fly. I think that such balance is necessary. Today, there is not a single appointed female minister in Lithuania. I know that there was an opportunity to appoint a competent and wonderful woman to the post of minister of ecology, but a man was nominated instead. On the other hand, we are not necessarily happy with the women currently in the *Seima*. Evidently, women themselves are not ready to take an active part in political life. I think that these things are beginning to change because a new generation is developing. We have many hopes for the future."

Doctor of Science Stanislava Domarkienė: "If a man or a woman of similar educational backgrounds is to be appointed to an executive post, the man is chosen in most cases. Why? Is it thought that the woman will not be competent? No. It is due to the lack of respect for women. It will be a long time before the opinion of an entire population can be changed. The fact that women's organizations have been established shows that there are problems in our society which must be solved. The question is, are such organizations equipped to handle them? The number of these organizations is not great, and they are not well-supported. Such organizations do draw attention to the numerous problems, but government legislators must also contribute."

Deputy Antanas Baskas: "Historical evidence discussed by Marija Alseikaitė Gimbutas claims that Lithuanian women are descended from a matrifocal culture. Domination by men prevents women from displaying their true characters. Our mode of life, determined by men, even compels women to go against nature and kill their unborn children. From 1987–1993, of all fourteen post-Communist countries, the number of people living in poverty increased most dramatically in Lithuania. In 1993, in Latvia and Poland, 25 percent of the population was living in poverty, but, in Lithuania, this figure was almost 50 percent. In Czech Republic, Hungary, Slovakia, and Slovenia, in this same year, less than 3 percent of the population was living below the poverty line. These

statistics show that there are different influences in all of these
countries."

Doctor of Social Science Žaneta Simanavičienė: "Do we need
a political association for women in Lithuania? We should certainly be political. Otherwise, women will not have a say in the
government. Men will take all the orator posts, and our voices we
will not be heard. Women in Lithuania are humiliated, underval-
ued, and have a role of third-rate importance. Everything is in the
hands of men, and, unfortunately, not the best ones."

Doctor Birutė Obelienienė: "Today's situation is such that
women no longer want to be mothers. The last bastion of our
national heritage—mother-love—is dying."

Businesswoman Régina Blazevičiutė: "It is very difficult for
women in business. It is impossible to get credit from the banks.
Figures from the labor exchange show that almost three-quarters of
unemployed persons are women!"

Pensioner Liučija Borisevičienė, living in poverty: "It was never
so bad as it is now. I receive a pension of 119 *litai* ($25) per month.
Expenses for my flat and telephone cost 72 *litai*. How am I supposed to live? I also have to take care of my disabled son, but, if
I did not have him, I would not live at all!"

Peasant Stanislava Buitkuvienė: "Agriculture has been ruined,
family farms have been destroyed, land has been taken away, and
the fruit of the earth is not being cultivated. Better produce is
bought from foreign countries, and our grain and potato seeds are
rotting . . . "

———

These excerpts are taken from meetings and conversations
with various people whom I met while traveling through Lithuania.
I visited many villages and towns, trying to understand what our
people live for, what our greatest problems are, and what solutions
can be found.

While there were—and are—many unions, associations, professional gatherings, and clubs for woman in Lithuania, their meaning is mostly symbolic. They do not have the political power nor
the potential to solve serious problems. They generally focus on
charitable work, self-education, and specific areas of study. Only
the deputies of the *Seima* (Parliament) have power to change the
absurd laws which are currently in force. For instance, there is

legislation which actually promotes monopolies and encourages corruption. Because of present laws, a candidate must be a member of an official political party in order to run for a seat in Parliament. This prerequisite forced us to form a political party which would represent the interests of women, children, and families.

I began to analyze the platforms of the major political parties in Lithuania, and I did not find any realistic moral support nor any hope for the future of our nation. I then decided that we must wake up and begin a movement for our rights. In 1993, in Düsseldorf, Germany, there was a convention, the theme of which was "Women Can Do Everything." While attending the convention, we learned about the self-expression enjoyed by Western European women, as well as about their right to take part in legislation and the governing of the State. We rejoiced to learn about the lives of independent women and we decided that there was no time to delay.

On 14 March 1993, my first article—"When Women Begin to Get Angry"—was published in the Lithuanian press. The words "Party of Women" were finally in print. I quote a portion of that article here because, when it was published, it caused a great deal of controversy.

> Executive men of the State are raving that they already "put" us into the capitalist system. Do you feel it, dear women? I would not say that they are lying. It is only that they live as if there were no starvation, no poverty, pressure and hatred, no avalanche of crimes and no wonderfully orchestrated corruption. Yes, the government officials live in the capitalist system, but maybe they live in the Communist system too? They use (free of charge) goods produced by all of us, and fling down leftovers from their tables as if we were little dogs at the mercy of the State "dispenser." Yes, they still have crumbs for the hungry and disobedient after using their whip. Under their skirts the predatory SODRA, who takes one third of everything, is flourishing and growing fat. Mr. Prime Minister himself acknowledges the predatory nature of SODRA but responds only with a helpless gesture of his elegant hands. Everyone in this country is helpless, incorporeal, and weightless . . . What folly . . . Big, tall, handsome, rich, fashionably dressed—men, men, men . . . Male companies . . . In this kingdom of male egos, the value of women is forgotten: woman-creator, woman-inspirer, woman-mother, woman-cherisher, and woman-peacemaker. Beauty and rest, peace and

honesty, love and selflessness are forgotten. No one seems to
need the intuition of the Lithuanian woman, her spirituality,
her heat for war and throne.

Women in our "free" Motherland are second-rate citizens: friends, maidservants, and concubines of men. The one
or two women who have risen above the grey crowd of men
were at once abused, spit on, and trampled because of their
logic, beauty, and intelligence. We only honor women who
are far away and cannot put the intellect and power of
Lithuanian men on trial . . .

Our country is in a catastrophic state. There are more
people dying than being born! Sixty percent of our citizens
believe that women's lives are more difficult than men's lives.
Men allocate most of the difficult work to women but do not
allow them to participate when important social issues are
being discussed. There are fewer and fewer women in government. There are more women university graduates than men,
but men hold the highest posts in education. There are one
and a half times more jobless women than men, and women
commit 10 times fewer crimes than men.

While women are bearing and raising children, men are
cultivating their careers. Men look at their friends from their
heights, triumphantly and proudly, while they flirt with their
colleagues or charming secretaries. Even capitalist women
(businesswomen, bankers, and entrepreneurs) are eyed with
suspicious contempt.

Until now women have been suffering and keeping silent, but these years of stupor are passing. Women are growing more and more brave and perceptive in their fight for Life.
This fight is going on all over the world. In Lithuania, honorable and wise women are emerging. They do not want to be
obedient workers anymore, instead they want to stand up tall
next to MAN, conqueror of the world!

Men are nagging one another to death and are destroy-
ing, little by little, our Motherland (which does not belong
only to them). Poverty, despair, joblessness, corruption, and
criminality are the babies carried in arms of tired Lithuanian
mothers, wives, sisters, and beloved women. When are things
going to change?

A week ago we, five representatives of the Lithuanian
Association of Women, participated in a congress organized by
Western-European women. In some Western European nations

40 percent of the governors are women. Women are important and have influence. Companies formed by women are flourishing. They seem to be as necessary in governing as their colleagues with trousers. They are protected by their Constitutions and hundreds of additional laws. Their lives are satisfied, wonderful, joyful, and rich. Their movements are honorable and influential. They address real problems and get things accomplished. Why are we still playing the role of silly sheep? Why do we let men jeer at us and at our natural right to equality? Women of Europe invite us to unite. Why don't we? Because in our government women have no authority, and yet it is our own fault. We are obedient, submissive, and accept the escapades of men like the tricks of adult boys. They are wasting millions earned by us for satisfying their caprices while our children have no medicine, go without decent food, study in schools of the Middle Ages, and are educated in the spirit of Communism. And we still keep silent! We kept silent when men squandered millions of dollars buying thermometers of bad quality, and later on we kept silent while they spent money to change Lithuanian passports because of the position of the horses tail in the State Emblem. We kept silent while they produced paper which was called Lithuanian currency and while money from other countries was forbidden.

The saddest thing is that our Motherland does not need us and our children anymore. The State is only interested in us for our usefulness to the State budget. The Prime Minister declares that he will protect Lithuanian markets "from cheap foreign goods." What is this, ignorance or the open mocking of Lithuanian people? Our President declares that we are already living in a capitalist system.

Our most popular telecast, "Yes and No" illustrated the great imperium of the Lithuanian mafia (and we again keep silent!). Maybe this really is capitalism. Yet I have traveled to other capitalist countries and this does not seem like capitalism to me. I do not condemn those who are leaving this hopeless country of hypocrites and cowards, but I have decided that I will do everything to ensure that my children and grandchildren will live in some little European town where I relax about their future. A Motherland which hates her children is condemned in the eyes of God. That is why we, who returned from the Dusseldorf Congress, are proposing this: Women wake up! If not us—who? If not today—when?"

I began riding around Lithuania and talking with women in cities, towns, and villages about the necessity to form a serious political organization of women which would protect our rights and our futures. For two years, I wrote articles and visited almost the entire country. Lithuanians have an allergy to the word *party* because, during the years of Soviet occupation, the concept of political parties was discredited. Despite this, almost all of the women to whom I spoke acknowledged the need for a women's party.

Everywhere, we are forming initiative groups, developing ideas, and creating a party platform. We believe that the Party of Women has the potential to bring harmony and awareness to political life in Lithuania, and that it will help to end the existing discrimination against women.

According to government statistics 41 percent of Lithuanian women do not want to change anything in the governing system, 23 percent think the country should be governed only by men, and 28 percent feel that many more women must take part in our government. I would challenge these statistics, because, in my meetings with women, not one them was indifferent to the future of their children. This future depends on general prosperity that is also moral, material, and spiritual. Intelligent, educated, sensitive, and intuitive women are needed in the government. They could help to govern our country in a more subtle and clever manner. Women should stand next to our men, not higher nor lower. A bird can fly only if it has both wings!

Women with different views and ideologies approved of the idea to form a Party of Women. It was discussed in the presidium of the Lithuanian Association of Women, and an initiative group was organized to prepare the statute and platform. On 25 February 1995, the Constituent Congress took place, and the party was officially founded. The former Prime Minister of Lithuania, Kazimiera Prunskienė, was elected as chairman of the party, and I was elected as chairman of the council. The general regulations of the party are as follows:

1. The Lithuanian Party of Women is an independent, volunteer, political organization which unites members to take part in political activities and solve problems. Activities of the LPW do not depend on State agencies nor on other political parties or movements. The Party works on the principle of equality of all its members.
2. LPW is a lawful body which has a seal and a current bank account.

3. The Party follows the Constitution of the Lithuanian Republic, other laws, and normative acts of the Lithuanian Republic, as well as the Republic's statutes in all of its activities.
4. Lithuanian citizens who concur with the statute can volunteer to join the Party.

Objectives and Goals

1. To establish a new nonpatriarchal environment in Lithuania in which competence and devotion to the problems of our people and the State, not sex, would decide the capacity in which citizens participated in political parties and the government.
2. To train women in self-expression, formalities, and responsibility concerning the workings of the State.
3. To develop an environment which would encourage the participation of women in political and government activities, as well as their nomination and election to all levels of government office.
4. To concentrate on realistic political activities, including culture of family, women, and children; health and social protection; and trying to solve general problems in our society.
5. To organize educational activities to enhance the understanding of democracy which will harmonize the role of women and men in society, economy, politics, and government.
6. To strive toward harmonious relations between the State and individuals.
7. To invent a new tradition of moral and responsible politics.

One of the primary objectives is to uphold the United Nations' Convention to Abolish All Forms of Discrimination Against Women, which states that women and men are equal under the law with freedom and equal economic, social, cultural, civil, and political rights.

As this is being written, serious preparations are underway for the 1997 elections. We are conducting studies, seminars, and weekends of self-education. We are also selecting candidates for the *Seima*, and preparing them for earnest political work.

Unfortunately, there are still men and (alas!) women for whom this Party seems to be ridiculous or strange, and who think that women should take part in the already existing political parties. They believe that women are overreacting. This creates a great deal of pressure and anxiety for women, and much uncertainty concerning the future of our movement.

Maximum attention will be paid to our list of candidates. We must be careful to chose candidates who are above criticism. While improper social and political actions by men are accepted or easily excused, these same actions would never be acceptable if done by a woman.

Concerning the ideological direction of the Party of Women, the current questions are basic. For example, people ask if our party is right or left. I answer that it is straight ahead.

Rather than simply generate an interest in politics, I hope to emphasize the importance of primary issues—namely, the well-being of our children, the stability of families, growth of the economy, and protection of our health and our nation's ecology.

Some colleagues suggest that these objectives sound more like the program of a women's organization than of a political party. I say, "This is not a club. It is party!" Yet, we became a party only because our splendid men tried to keep elections to the *Seima* closed to us. They decided that the country can be governed only by the members of parties. So, we became members of a party. Now, we must patiently learn everything that will be useful in developing noble politics. We will have to translate our dreams and our work into an ideological framework.

While I have studied the tenets of many political schools of thought, classic liberalism has made the greatest impression on me. This "religion of party" was revered by the greatest sons of Lithuania, and it could still serve us today. The renowned slogan originated during the French revolutions: "Freedom, Equality, Brotherhood."

Freedom is the independence of the individual from the dictates of the government or ideology. Equality is being equal to all in the presence of God and the law. Brotherhood is respecting the freedom of other persons. Liberalism, which seems more like a philosophy, respects culture, art, education, and property. I hope that the Council agrees with me, and that, one day, we will announce that LPW is following the principles of classical liberalism.

Those who are mocking call us the "party of sex!" There are, however, already eight men in our party, and their numbers will increase. Our door is open to everyone who respects women and acknowledges the equality of the sexes.

There are still so many problems to be addressed! Infant and child mortality is increasing. Teenage crime has increased by 400 percent in the last four years. Hospitals, schools, and kindergartens are impoverished. On every corner, a beggar is sitting. Young men are murdering children, and women are being raped. Despair and horror have returned to the hearts of our people.

Government? State? What can they do if they waste all their time squabbling about their own interests? We are longing for intelligent and moral politicians and competent governors. We cannot be silent anymore.

Members of my family, my friends, and my colleagues have warned me many times that this movement would not bring me peace and joy. They warned that I would be "plucked and X-rayed by the nation," and that tomatoes and stones would be thrown at me. I have already experienced the beginning of this scrutiny.

People ask me, "You are living well. Why do you need all of this?" I respond, "I want all the women of Lithuania to live as well as I live." I believe that this is something worth fighting for. I hope that the *Seima* elections will have a good result. As many as 20 to 30 percent of the representatives could be women. Then, I could leave my post to a younger, more educated, multilingual, professional politician, and I would retire with a calm conscience.

I would like to write two more books, to begin educating my granddaughter, to grow flowers, and to travel. Politics is not my calling, and having stones thrown at me is not my pleasure. However, today, I know I must do something if I do not want my children and grandchildren to damn me tomorrow for my indifference.

I must shout, "Do not be afraid to be a woman! It is not all duty and sacrifice. It is a great happiness to be the creator, the inspiration, the custodian, and to stand tall next to men as equals."

Chapter 9

Moving Forward:
Women's Studies and Organizations

Marija Aušrinė Pavilionienė

INTRODUCTION

During our current transition period—and as Lithuanians look forward to the future and also reminisce and romanticize about the Lithuanian renaissance of the 1920s and 1930s—the status of women is at a crossroad. Traditional views can shackle women to family roles and inhibit their growth as productive citizens. There is, now, an urgent need to understand the historical and sociological reasons for discrimination against women, and to envision alternative ways in which women can contribute to society in the future. However, without data relating to the moral, psychological, physical, political, and economic oppression, there will be no interest nor any action to end this negative sex bias. Without awareness of discrimination against women—and discrimination against men as well—there will be no hope for policies of equal social, political, and economic opportunity in this country. In order to recover from an era of devastation under the Soviet regime, the potential of women must be cultivated and utilized.

WOMEN'S STUDIES

During this crucial transition period, the importance of women's studies is paramount. The women's movement and the meaning of women's studies has not been properly understood nor has it been appreciated in our society.

First, and foremost, most people simply do not understand the concept. We attempt to explain that feminist insights can be useful in almost every branch of science. Feminist studies are a woman's right to a perspective which examines and explains women's experiences in a patriarchal society. The feminist perspective offers a critical evaluation of academic theories which analyze women's subjugation, their physiology, their psychology, and their roles within the family and society.

Some male academics maintain that, in Lithuania, the women's movement and women's studies create an artificial isolation between the sexes. They forget that, in the past, it was men who distanced themselves from women, considering them to be the "second sex." At the same time, our Western sisters and enlightened Lithuanian women voluntarily support even separation of the sexes, at least temporarily, in order to find their own voice.

Lithuanian men should be proud that women are awakening, and they should support their efforts to contribute to society rather than crush their struggle with irony, skepticism and empty words. They think that the Women's Studies Centre is a women's citadel where men are unwanted and unwelcome. Not one man at Vilnius University has expressed any interest in assisting or collaborating with research or seminars at the Centre.

THE WOMEN'S STUDIES CENTRE

In 1570, Vilnius University began as a Jesuit college with two faculties: philosophy and theology. In 1989, after being closed for two-hundred years by the Czarist and Soviet regimes, the Faculty of Philosophy, which houses the social sciences, reopened. At first, the age and tradition of Vilnius University seem to be incompatible with the concept of women's studies. It is a strange juxtaposition of the past and present, the dynamics of which are noteworthy. Vilnius University is situated in the most cosmopolitan city in Lithuania, which offers an abundance of world views, with the potential for polemics and meaningful dialogues. In such an environment, one would think that women's studies would be welcomed as a new discipline and theoretical perspective. Unfortunately, this has not been our experience.

The Women's Centre was set up in May 1992 on the initiative of the Lithuanian Association of University Women. It is an independent interdisciplinary center. One of the most important goals of LAUW was to establish a place of enlightenment where academic and research activities would help to change Lithuanian stereotypes of sex, gender, and family. We hoped to disseminate ideas of sexual equality and promote policies encouraging equal opportunity.

I prepared a proposal for the Centre, which was then discussed by the LAUW Board of Association, and later approved by the University Senate. Dr. Giedrė Purvaneckienė was appointed as director of the Women's Centre.

After formation of the Centre was approved, university space was allocated, but no funding was allotted. Thus, for the first year of existence, the Centre functioned without any financial support. During the second year, 2,500 *litas* ($622) was designated for the Centre from the university budget.

The Women's Studies Centre was established with an interdisciplinary focus, and it has the potential to create an extensive feminist academic and research network. However, most of those who lecture at the Centre have no special training in women's studies. Lack of trained scholars, and a dearth of feminist literature, have made curriculum development at the Centre very difficult. Our scholars need books to understand feminist theory and research, to compare women's experiences from different countries, and to find a place for Lithuanian women in a global context.

The hunger for books free of Marxist/Leninist ideology was sorely felt during the fifty years of Soviet occupation, and, to date, only a handful of feminist books has been published in Lithuania. Several articles on women's issues have been published in various Lithuanian periodicals, and translations from the writings of Christine de Pisan, Mary Wollstonecraft, John Mill, Simone de Beauvoir, and Julia Kristeva have appeared in popular journals. The lack of feminist literature leaves lecturers and students at a grave disadvantage. The Centre has started a library of English, German, French, and Scandinavian feminist literature, but in-depth awareness of feminist discourse is available only to those who are fluent in other languages.

During the 1992–93 academic year, we were able to offer only two multidisciplinary courses—"Women and Culture," and "Women and Society." However, we also sponsored two seminars; "The

Concept of Woman in the History of Western Culture" and "The Letter as a Feminine Mode of Communication."

In our efforts to expand the curriculum during the 1993–1994 academic year, the Centre engaged staff from other faculties and departments, as well as lecturers from other institutions. We offered "Women and Men in Western European and American Literature of the nineteenth and twentieth Centuries," "Archetypes in the Psychology of C. G. Jung," and "Gender Relations in Society." During both semesters, our teaching staff was augmented with foreign professors: Suzanne Lie from Norway, Inger Lovkrona from Sweden, and Dean Johnson from the United States.

In the fall of 1994, the Centre started a two-year curriculum, and added "Women in Lithuanian Literature," "The Psychology and Physiology of Women," "The Social Aspects of Health," "The Status of Women in the Great Duchy of Lithuania," "Feminist Literary Criticism," "Postmodernism and Feminism in Lithuania, "Sociology of Women's Work," "Phenomenology of Women's Existence," and "Women's Rights and Freedoms."

The three years of the Centre's existence have demonstrated that students, and women of LAUW, take a great interest in the Centre's activities. However, other departments seem wary of our efforts. Although they encourage their students to participate, the older generation of academics at the university do not seem interested in feminist ideas. It is the students who are making the first steps "to enter the mine field."

Students from a variety of disciplines are eager to know more about gender and women's issues. The attendance of students confirms that they want to explore new ideas and perspectives, and they are seeking alternatives to the traditional opportunities available in the past. This year, about one-hundred students from different faculties have taken separate courses. However, only three students elected to the 2-year program. This low number reflects the fact that a degree in women's studies would not provide a student with career possibilities in Lithuania. We are, however, proud to have our first doctorate student, Asta Markevičiutė, who has chosen feminist literary criticism and Canadian women's literature as her doctoral thesis topic.

The present university administration supports the idea of the Women's Studies Centre, and considers the Centre to be part of the reform efforts and democratization. However, we face the insecurity of being a low priority, and we are subject to budget cuts. Therefore, the Centre has no guarantees that lectures and studies will continue. Then, too, change of university administration could mean the closure of the Centre.

Because of low wages and uncertainty about the Centre's future, our scholars must combine other professional activities with their work at the Centre. Enlightened women, who work on a voluntary basis, help to stir interest in the problems faced by women—and by the Centre—and initiate research on vital issues. The growth of women's studies would be greater if women from other departments could work at our Centre full-time. However, economically this is not an option.

Financially, the university is unable to allot substantial support to the Centre because the government does not provide the money promised in the university budget. Only 15 percent of the university budget comes from student tuition, renting of university premises, and income from various contracts. For the rest, we depend on government funding.

In 1994, twenty-nine million *litas* was to be given for the maintenance of the university. However, we received only 24 million *litas*. The aged university buildings are also its architectural monuments. For their preservation, the university needs seven million per year. In 1993, we received only three million. In 1994, it was 1.5 million, and, in 1995, only one million *litas* was allocated for architectural maintenance. Under such circumstances, it is untenable for the Centre to expect much financial support. We cannot help but lament that, despite the importance of our historical buildings, the Lithuanian woman's soul and spirit also need restoration after a long era of oppression under the Soviet regime.

Presently, the Centre has three full-time employees—a department head, a librarian, and a secretary. In 1994, the budget for the Centre was 2,500 *litas* ($622). Compare this to the faculty of economics, allotted 120,850 *litas;* the faculty of law, which received 44,140 *litas;* and the 45,100 *litas* that the mathematics faculty received.

Lack of interest and support from the government is very discouraging. Twice, the Centre has tried to join the Tempus Program for Eastern Europe, an international network that allows students and faculty to study in member countries. Both times, our proposals were rejected because our government would not allot the available foreign funds for this particular project. On a more hopeful note, Prime Minister Adolfas Slezevičius has promised the leaders of the Lithuanian women's organizations financial support for women's research projects. We hope that this promise comes to fruition.

The Centre has many plans from the future. We hope to investigate widowhood, senility, serial marriage, and divorce. Our future might be uncertain, but we will continue our efforts to educate and enlighten Lithuanians to the best of our ability.

The Centre is grateful to various foreign institutions and organizations that have supported our work through ideas, advice, programs, books, journals, and grants which have allowed researchers to travel abroad to women's conferences and meetings. The Open Lithuanian Foundation has helped the Centre acquire computer and copying equipment, and has also allotted funds for feminist journals. In 1994, the United Nations' resident coordinator in Lithuania allocated funds for two research projects: "The Value Orientation of Lithuanian Women," granted to Dr. Giedrė Purvaneckienė; and "The Professional and Social Mobility of Lithuanian Women, granted to Dr. Vida Kanopienė. In 1995, the Democracy Commission Program of the American Embassy in Vilnius awarded the Centre two grants for future research projects: "Violence Against Women in Lithuania," awarded to this writer; and "Discrimination of Women in the Labor Market," awarded to Dr. Kanopienė.

The Lithuanian government has contributed 4,000 *litas* to the "violence against women" project. In Lithuania, data concerning incidents of sexual and domestic violence has been officially registered only since 1994. This crucial topic has received wide public attention, due to the women's movement, activities of the Women's Home Organization, and our Centre. The first seminar devoted to this problem, and organized by various women associations, was held in May 1995. We also held an International Conference on Gender and Literature in that same month, to encourage fiction as a vehicle for feminist ideas—a medium to which people easily respond.

POLITICAL POWER

In Lithuania, the women's movement—and especially women's struggles to find a political voice—is still openly ridiculed. To date, Lithuanian women have not played any considerable role in politics. Those who have managed to reach the heights of power for a short time—such as former Prime Minister Kazimiera Prunskienė, former Deputy Nijolė Oželytė, and Deputy Zita Slicytė—are remembered more for their personal traits, rather than their political accomplishments. Moreover, their efforts toward improving women's lives were negligible. They have been criticized for their inability to hear others' opinions, and their lack of tolerance and over-confidence. Because of these cases, personal characteristics have marred the image of women in politics, and these points have been used as "proof" of women's unsuitability for political positions.

Most men consider women to be inferior, and they lack confidence in their abilities to tackle political, economic, and social problems. More importantly, many Lithuanian women have no interest in politics. They favor motherhood and professional work over political involvement. They identify political action with masculine behavior, power struggles, private property disputes, corruption, and hypocrisy.

Men, as the "ruling class," enthusiastically support the patriarchal traditions of the Catholic Church. The resurgence in the popularity of the Catholic Church has been accompanied by the glorification of motherhood. This is evidenced by the re-commemoration of Mother's Day on 7 May. This replaces the Soviet holiday of International Women's Day. On the one hand, this represents a purge of "things Soviet." On the other hand, it is a revealing statement concerning the perception of women's role in our society.

The irony of this symbolic reconstruction is clear. It is impossible to negate that every mother is a woman. However, this glorification of motherhood does not bring mothers financial support for their children and many Lithuanian children, suffer the consequences.

Lithuanian women had great hopes regarding the newly formed Women's Party which was set up in 1995. It is a pity that the platform of the Party—conceived by K. Prunskienė, V. Apanavičienė, B. Grinbėrgienė, Z. Pagirskienė—centers on the criticism of current social, economic, and political policies, rather than offering concrete proposals on ways to change the many difficulties which our society now faces.

The party promises to enrich politics with "Christian values and humanistic striving," and overcome "the inherited backwardness and the crisis of the transitional period which is typical of all Eastern European countries." Their stated goal is to make politics "a rational and humane compromise between oppositional groups." However well-meaning, they might be, these vague promises echo the empty rhetoric of the Communist Party. Furthermore, it is difficult to understand how the Women's Party will become "a rational compromise" when, in Lithuania, the political, social, and moral discrimination of women is so vivid.

The Women's Party defines itself as "the party of maternal and nonpatriarchal culture." While this might reflect women's best interests, it is difficult to believe that this political party will be able to turn back the hand of time to the period of supposed matriarchy in Lithuanian culture.

We hope, however, that this party will help to adjust the imbalance of sexual power in government and politics, and assist in forming the basis for a new culture of communication between the sexes. However, the reality of the party's performance has been disappointing. It has split into two conflicting groups, and we have yet to see any results from the party's activity.

WOMEN'S ORGANIZATIONS

In Lithuania during these four years of independence, thirty-three women's organizations have been set up or reestablished. This is an impressive number, if one compares it with the National Women's Council which existed during Soviet times. The Women's Council was controlled by the Communist Party, and it embodied the facade ideology of the Soviet regime. It presented the same illusions put forth in Soviet propaganda—that is, "The citizens of the Soviet Union are equal; happily living in a prosperous country, and struggling for peace and a better future."

In contrast, current government institutions do not encourage or support these women's organizations which are voluntary organizations trying to "patch up the holes" in Lithuanian society. Women's organizations address legal, educational, social, ethical, and moral issues. Among them are The Society of Mothers of Lithuanian Soldiers, The Widows' Association, The Women's Home, The Association of Lithuanian Businesswomen, The Women's League, The Lithuanian Society of Polish Women, The Lithuanian Society of Catholic Women, The Lithuanian Society of Christian Democratic Women, and many others. Each, in its own way fights against legal, social, and moral injustice.

CONCLUSION

One can discuss the women's status in Lithuania from many aspects. However, one fact is undisputable. The country needs a comprehensive examination of the women's situation. A progressive educational program concerning issues of family, sex, and gender issues would be beneficial to both women and men. The time has come to end discrimination against women in Lithuania.

Feminist lecturers and researchers are well aware that scientific data regarding specific topics is much easier to obtain than is achieving social change and reform in the minds of men and women living in this traditionally Catholic country. We believe that the Centre undertakes the important responsibility of the educating the younger generation. We want to enhance their intellectual perspectives, and to help them understand that many honored Lithuanian traditions—such as, the father as bread winner, the mother as caretaker of the family hearth—can simultaneously elevate and oppress both sexes.

Chapter 10

Modern Women in Lithuania

Renata Guobužaitė

Lithuanian women are having difficulty adapting to the new economic and political situations. Our experience from the Soviet period has not provided us with the necessary skills to cope in today's world. For many years, we have been forced for many years to look East, and, now, we are told to look West. We cannot, however, simply import Western ideas and role models and apply them to our changing realities. Instead, we must find original solutions to our problems.

Independence has initiated many positive changes in our economic, political, and social arenas. However, the lives of women have not improved.

Women's unemployment and the feminization of poverty are two major problems in our country. In addition, our abortion rates are high. Domestic violence is frequent, and is still being treated as a private problem. Thirty-three percent of Lithuanian women have been badly beaten, 20 percent have experienced rape or attempted rape, and 18 percent have been robbed (Purvaneckienė 1994).

The situation is critical, but this is a very propitious moment to change it. New laws are being passed. New images are forming, and new activities are available. Our society is presently open and receptive to change. It is a great opportunity for women to get involved and be successful in all areas of life, including politics, business, and the public domain.

Despite these opportunities, it seems that women are being left behind in our society. According to a recent survey, about 75 percent of the women questioned stated that they would prefer staying at home and being housewives to going into the work force (Janulevičiūtė 1995). The number of women working in management and administration has decreased by 27 percent since 1980 (Lietuvos Statistikos Metrastis 1995). Women's diminished participation in public life and the labor market can be found in all post-Communist countries. How can we explain this trend? I would argue that the two major reasons for this trend are historical and current, and both relate to patriarchy and discrimination against women.

The first reason is that, during the Soviet period, women were overworked. The last two generations of Lithuanian women were forced to work. Of course, this presented some opportunities for women. They were financially independent, had the opportunity to socialize at work, and have careers. No one seemed to notice that in addition to their jobs, women retained the traditional duties of wife and mother.

They had a double, or even triple, work day, working full-time, hurrying home, cooking, cleaning, caring for the children, and spending lots of time waiting in long lines to buy basic necessities. As worker, wife, mother, consumer, and cook, women had too many responsibilities. Yet, they heroically tried to fulfill them. There was not much time for hobbies, leisure, or dreams. This stressful existence had damaging psychological and professional effects on women.

Now, after that long period of hard work, they have, for the first time, the opportunity to choose what they want to do. Given this history, it is no wonder that women are likely to skip the working world, in order to have more time for themselves and their families.

The second reason for women's current prejudice against work is that they are not faring well in today's labor market. The labor market has changed dramatically from what it was during the Soviet period when jobs were all but guaranteed. Now, the market economy does not guarantee employment as did the welfare state.

Given all the economic difficulties in Lithuania, the situation is dismal. Many qualified people have lost their jobs, or are having trouble finding jobs. Their knowledge and skills are different from what is required in today's labor market. Almost two-thirds of all unemployed people are women, and the hardest hit are older women

(Purvaneckienė 1995). As they approach pensionable age, women suffer the worst discrimination in the labor market.

Young women face different problems. In Lithuania, women usually marry very young, and many women are pregnant when they get married or become pregnant shortly after marriage (Department of Statistics 1995). Child care and domestic responsibilities usually fall to the mother. Women spend the crucial career years taking care of their families instead of getting an education or qualifications for a good job. Several years later, when the children start school, women might want to enter, or return to, the labor market, only to find that they cannot compete with experienced workers. Thus, young women accept lower paying jobs, when they find work at all.

Young women also face serious sexual discrimination in the labor market. Many employers are unwilling to employ young women. Our legal system provides some benefits to pregnant women, women with small children, and single mothers. They are eligible for some subsidies, additional vacation days, and a shorter work day. Although these policies were created to protect women, employers find them to be burdensome, and they actually promote discrimination.

Feeling unwanted and discriminated against, women look for security elsewhere. They turn to tradition, and retreat into the family. Women have many problems concerning the labor market and the family. It is difficult to find the right way to solve these problems. Lithuanian women cannot use Western models, because our Soviet experience, coupled with serious economic problems, make our situation different from that in the West. This could explain why Lithuanians encounter feminist ideas with a lack of faith, and they view feminism as a Western phenomenon based on Western philosophy.

Lithuanian women are confused. They cannot live as they did before because the economic, political, and social situations have changed. On the other hand, they cannot simply adopt Western ideas and models. There are no ready-made solutions, and it is difficult for Lithuanian women to decide how to live. Some of them will choose business or work. Some will choose education. Some will choose family, and some will try to combine these endeavors. Only the future will tell how successful these choices will be.

Lithuanian women are at a decisive moment in their lives. They are responsible for creating a new positive image of intelligent and active women in our society. They must take the best from their own experiences, and combine that with what we now can learn from the West. Our entire society will profit if women can find the right balance and path.

REFERENCES

Department of Statistics
   1995. *Lithuanian Women*. Vilnius: Lithuanian Department of Statistics.

Janulevičiūtė, Birute
   1995. "Moteris ir Vyras—Paukštis su Dviem Sparnais."
   Kauno Diena, 10 January 1995.

Lietuvos Statistikos Metrastis
   1995. Vilnius: Information Center.

Purvaneckienė, Giedrė
   1994. "Woman's World." Newsletter of the Lithuanian
   preparatory committee of the IV World Conference on
   Women. Vilnius.

Chapter 11

Marija Gimbutas:
Tribute to a Lithuanian Legend

Joan Marler

In June 1993, archaeologist Marija Gimbutas made her last visit to her Motherland of Lithuania. From the moment she emerged from passport control, the television cameras were rolling, press cameras were clicking, and a throng of family and friends swept her into their embrace.

That evening the television news exclaimed that Marija Gimbutas had arrived—and, throughout the two and a half weeks of her visit, there were daily articles in the press, television coverage of her lectures and interviews, documentary filming, and meetings with colleagues, students, family, and friends.

Marija Gimbutas had returned, as a world-famous scholar, to receive an honorary doctorate from Vytautas Magnus University in Kaunas where, fifty-five years earlier, her studies of archaeology began. She was honored by President Brazauskas in a splendid ceremony that was reported to the nation.

Although Dr. Gimbutas was critically ill with cancer, she was radiant from this unfettered outpouring of love and appreciation. While each previous visit to her homeland renewed her vitality, this journey celebrated the fulfillment of an extraordinary life.

Who was this woman—this diminutive scientist, whose prodigious accomplishments include the publication of more than twenty books, republished in numerous languages, and more than three hundred articles on European prehistory? How is it possible that such esoteric research could inspire the lives of countless individuals—not only in Lithuania, but throughout the world?

Some of her conclusions have generated a storm of controversy within her own field of archaeology (Steinfels 1990). Nevertheless, mythologist Joseph Campbell compared Gimbutas's work with Champollion's decipherment of Egyptian hieroglyphics (Campbell 1989, xiii), and anthropologist Ashley Montagu considers her findings to be as important as Schliemann's excavation of Troy. He writes, "Marija Gimbutas has given us a veritable Rosetta Stone of the greatest heuristic value for future work in the hermeneutics of archaeology and anthropology."[1]

EARLY LIFE

Marija Gimbutas was devoted to scientific achievement and creativity. She was sustained, throughout her life, by a complex stream of cultural, intellectual and spiritual influences that were deeply rooted in her identity as a Lithuanian, and in her abiding love for the land and the ancient culture.

During the nineteenth century in Lithuania, a vigorous intelligentsia arose from the peasant class, stimulated by the systematic suppression of traditional culture wrought by a century of Czarist rule. After the Lithuanian language was banned, Marija's mother's family became "book carriers" who risked imprisonment or deportation for smuggling Lithuanian books over the borders to be distributed by an underground network. Education was embraced as essential for cultural and political liberation.

Marija's parents, Veronika Janulaitytė-Alseikienė and Danielius Alseikas, were both medical doctors and active revolutionaries devoted to the rebirth of Lithuania. In 1918, the first year of independence from Russia, they established the first Lithuanian hospital in Vilnius. By the time Marija Birutė Alseikaitė was born on 23 January 1921, the Vilnius area was tormented by Polish occupation.

Marija's childhood home was an important center for political resistance and the preservation of Lithuanian culture. Dr. Alseika was, not only a physician, but a historian and publisher of a newspaper, *Vilniaus Žodis,* and the cultural magazine *Vilniaus Šviesa.* He was also a respected leader in the struggle for independence from Poland.[2]

Dr. Alseikienė was considered to be a "miracle worker," an oculist who restored people's sight through cataract operations.

She was also a cultural activist who supported the preservation of Lithuanian folk arts. The finest traditional and contemporary artists, musicians, and writers met in their home.

I had the opportunity to get acquainted with writers and artists such as Vydunas, Vaižgantas, even Basanavičius, who was taken care of by my parents. When I was four or five years old, I would sit in Basanavičius's easy chair and I would feel fine. And later, throughout my entire life, Basanavičius's collected folklore remained extraordinarily important for me.[3]

When Marija was ready for formal education, she attended a liberal school with the children of other Lithuanian intellectuals. She also received private tutelage in music and languages, and was nurtured by an extended family that included her brother, Vytautas; her cousin, Meilė; and her beloved Aunt Julija, a dentist, who was like a second mother. The vital intensity of that environment promoted a devotion to political and aesthetic freedom, intellectual achievement, and a tenacious originality.

From the very beginning the children had total freedom. We were free to create our own individualities although work for our nation and education always came first. We went to the theater and to concerts as a natural way of life. Without that we couldn't live from the earliest years.[4]

Lithuania was one of the last European countries to be Christianized, and many ancient traditions were still alive into the twentieth century. Marija's exposure to this rich but vanishing heritage was encouraged from an early age.[5]

In our house were the Fates . . . of a continuous pagan tradition. All my servants believed in them. They were real—spinning the thread of human life . . .[6]

The folklore and mythological imagery that Marija absorbed reflected, not only the Indo-European pantheon of sky gods, but a much earlier bond with the Earth and her mysterious cycles that was still alive in the Lithuanian countryside.

The rivers were sacred, the forest and trees were sacred, the hills were sacred. The earth was kissed and prayers were said every morning, every evening . . .[7]

The balance of male and female powers, as expressed in the folk material, had its correspondence in people's daily lives:

> Officially the patriarchal system is clearly dominating, but in reality, there is an inheritance from Old Europe in which the woman is the center. In some areas the matrilineal system really exists, such as in my family. I don't see that the sons were more important.[8]

Blissful summers were spent with the plants and animals at her mother's farm near Vilnius. In the fields nearby, people still did their work in traditional ways.

> The old women used sickles and sang while they worked. The songs were very authentic, very ancient. At that moment I fell in love with what is ancient because it was a deep communication and oneness with Earth. I was completely captivated. This was the beginning of my interest in folklore.[9]

In 1931, Marija's parents separated, and she moved to Kaunas with her mother and brother. To be parted from her father, and from Vilnius, was her first great sadness. Then, when she was fifteen, her father suddenly died. Marija turned inward, as a response to this shock, and vowed to continue her father's life.

> All of a sudden I had to think what I shall be, what I shall do with my life. I had been so reckless in sports—swimming for miles, skating, bicycle riding. I changed completely and began to read...[10]

At that point, Marija's life as a dedicated scholar began. The death of her father kindled a deep desire to investigate all that could be known about ancient origins, especially beliefs concerning death and prehistoric burial rites.

Marija poured over the work of Dr. Jonas Basanavičius, her "adopted grandfather," whose folklore collections were treasures of a vanishing Lithuanian heritage. She was motivated by the knowledge that such important research was part of her personal lineage. At ages sixteen and seventeen, she participated in ethnographic expeditions with other students to southeastern Lithuania. She was excited to make her own contributions to the preservation of this precious material. While the boys collected tools, Marija recorded folklore and songs. The many folk songs and stories she collected are preserved in the folklore archive of Vilnius University.

After graduating from high school with honors in 1938, Marija began studying at Vytautas Magnus University in Kaunas. In the meantime, enormous political forces were roiling. Following the German invasion of Poland in 1939, Vilnius was released from Polish occupation. Marija immediately left Kaunas, enrolled in the newly reorganized University of Vilnius, and became part of a spontaneous outpouring of cultural and educational reform initiated by the citizenry and the new government.

Encouraged by Professor Jonas Puzinas to study prehistory, in both Kaunas and Vilnius, Marija began to develop a complex, philosophical approach to archaeology and Baltic prehistory that was highly interdisciplinary. She studied ethnology and folklore with Jonas Balys and Juozas Baldžius, linguistics with Pranas Skardžius and Antanas Salys, and history with Ignas Jonynas and Levas Karsavinas. In early 1940, she spent several months recording folklore from the refugees of Byelorussia who were flooding into Vilnius.

The pioneer spirit of the young generation could not prevent the devastation brought by the Soviet invasion of 1940. All that the people had worked to create was destroyed. The Lithuanian government was deposed, the universities were taken over by Stalinists, innumerable books were burned, and thousands of people were deported to Siberia. As soon as the deportations began, Marija returned to Kaunas and hid in the forest with her mother near their small cottage. Many members of her own family and close friends were tortured, deported, or killed.

Marija joined the underground resistance movement, and she took part in the Lithuanian uprising of 1941 that helped to push out the Soviet forces. Soon afterward, the horrors of the German occupation began. In the midst of this chaos, Marija married her fiance, Jurgis Gimbutas.

In June 1942, Marija Gimbutas completed her master's studies in archaeology at the University of Vilnius, with secondary studies in folklore and comparative philology. Portions of her dissertation, "Life after Death in the Beliefs of Prehistoric Lithuania," were published in the Kaunas journal *Gimtasai Krastas*. She immediately began the preparation of her doctoral thesis.

In 1943, first while pregnant, and then caring for her newborn under conditions of occupation, Marija published eleven articles on the Balts and prehistoric burial rituals in Lithuania. Her cousin, Dr. Meilė Lukšienė, describes Marija during this period. "She was writing her first book about burial practices with one hand and rocking her first daughter Danutė with the other hand. Marija was a person of incredible will and organization."[11]

> That clearly kept me sane. I had something like a double life. I was happy doing my work; that was why I existed. Life just twisted me like a little plant, but my work was continuous in one direction.[12]

Because Vilnius University was closed by the Germans in 1943, Marija submitted her doctoral dissertation to the faculty of Humanitarian Sciences which was operating underground. The war conditions, however, prevented her from defending her thesis publicly.

THE ROAD OF TRIALS

While the Soviet front advanced for the second time on Lithuania in 1944, Marija, Jurgis, and baby Danutė took refuge with her mother at the small cottage near Kaunas. They also hid two Jewish women, despite the fact that Lithuanians who were found to be sheltering Jews were executed in public.[13]

On 8 July of that year, Marija and Jurgis escaped in a crowded barge on the Nemunas River. Marija, then 23, held her dissertation under one arm and Danutė in the other.

The rest of the war years were spent in Austria and Germany, under difficult conditions. Immediately after the war, in September 1945, Marija enrolled at Tübingen University. Six months later she received her Doctor of Philosophy degree in archaeology with emphases on prehistory, ethnology, and the history of religions. Her thesis, *Die Bestattung in Litauen in der vorgeschichtlichen Zeit*, which she translated into German, was published in Tübingen that same year. Although the subject of this thesis was archaeological, the reconstruction of burial rites was based on folklore, ethnology, and mythology, showing parallels with rites of other cultures.

In 1947, the second daughter, Živilė, was born. Because Marija was no longer a student, the young family was forced to move out of Tübingen into a nearby town where other Lithuanian refugees were living together. Nevertheless, she continued doing research at Tübingen University's library, and at the universities of Heidelberg and Munich. Meanwhile, Jurgis completed his doctorate in engineering at the University of Stuttgart. They worked together to send copies of Marija's book to universities, libraries, and consulates throughout the world, so that her scholarship would be known. By the time the Gimbutas family emigrated to America on 21 March 1949, Marija had published nearly thirty articles on Lithuanian prehistory, and had completed research for *Ancient Symbolism of Lithuanian Folk Art* which was published in Philadelphia in 1958.

Jurgis immediately found employment in Boston as an engineer. His mother, Elena, came with them and took care of the children, while Marija initially worked as a maid and at other menial jobs, all the while continuing her research.

A few months after their arrival in the United States, Marija presented herself at Harvard University. Recognized for her knowledge of most Eastern and Western European languages, she was encouraged to translate archaeological publications and, eventually, to write texts on the prehistory of Eastern and Central Europe.

> I had such a strong determination that I started right away to do research ... For three years, I wasn't given any money. I felt like a drowning person.[14]

She eventually received support from the Bollingen and Wenner-Gren Foundations for the preparation of *Prehistory of Eastern Europe*, which was published by Harvard University in 1956. This was the beginning of a series of fellowships and prestigious awards that assisted her ongoing work.

In 1954, the third daughter, Rasa, was born, and, in the following year, Marija Gimbutas was named a research fellow of Harvard's Peabody Museum, which is a lifetime honor. The annual report to the president of Harvard on the activities of the Peabody Museum for 1954–1955 states:

> [Dr. Gimbutas's] study of the prehistory of European Russia and the lands along the shore of the Baltic will be a classic which will stand for many years as an outstanding reference work. ... No such synthesis has ever been attempted, even by the Russians, and the whole subject is known to prehistorians in the rest of Europe only in a fragmentary and confused state ...[15]

THE FRUITFUL YEARS

With her extraordinary linguistic skills, Marija Gimbutas was in a unique position to develop an encyclopedic overview of European archaeology. During thirteen years of intensive research at Harvard, Marija Gimbutas studied every report on European archaeology, in its original language, that came into the Peabody Library, which she considered to be the best library for archaeologists in the world.

As her mother tongue, Lithuanian, is one of the most conservative of the Indo-European languages, and is similar to Sanskrit, the question of the origin of Proto-Indo-European speakers was always in her mind. Marija Gimbutas, therefore, became the first scholar to link linguistic research with available archaeological data to identify the homeland of the patriarchal people whom she called "Kurgans," and to trace their infiltrations into Europe.

> Linguists were talking about the Indo-European origins, and this influenced me, of course. The origin had to be the steppe region [of Russia]. *This was the first linguistic solution.*[16]

An early version of her "Kurgan Hypothesis" was presented at the International Congress of Ethnological Sciences in Philadelphia in 1956, which established a substantial point of departure for research in both fields. A further development of this hypothesis, with a revised chronology, was presented in 1966 at the Third Indo-European Conference, which was also held in Philadelphia.

The Prehistory of Eastern Europe was well distributed, and Dr. Gimbutas was soon recognized internationally as a rising star. She began to travel and lecture extensively throughout Western and Eastern Europe.

"I first saw Marija in 1958 in Hamburg," recalls Irish archaeologist Michael Herity, "and she was a truly beautiful woman . . ." She had a magnetic presence, a contagious enthusiasm for her work and "a devouring passion to search for meaning" which stimulated a vigorous exchange of ideas with colleagues throughout the world.[17] Friendships were formed during these years that continued throughout her life.

Although Marija Gimbutas lived and worked for forty-five years in America, the preservation of her Lithuanian heritage was always of central importance. In Boston, she helped to establish a Saturday School to teach Lithuanian language and culture, which was attended by all three daughters, and both she and Jurgis were very active in promoting the artistic life of the Lithuanian community. Later, she played a leading role in the advancement of Baltic Studies and was on the editorial boards of *Metmenys*, *Ponto-Baltica* and *Comparative Civilizations Review*—as well as other publications. She also contributed to *Lietuvių enciklopedija*, the *Quarterly Review of Archaeology*, and was the editor of the Eastern European archaeological section of *Encyclopedia Britanniea*.

By 1959, Marija Gimbutas had published nearly seventy articles in the Lithuanian, English, and German languages on Baltic archaeology and cultural history. Yet, not one monographic study of Baltic prehistory appeared in either Lithuania or Latvia during this period.[18]

During the first decade after her escape from Lithuania, Marija had no communication with her mother.

> I was afraid that if the Communist regime found out that my mother was receiving letters from her daughter in America, she could have been arrested and tortured—even killed. We all knew that. People were shipped to Siberia just because of things like that. So for ten years she had no idea if I was dead or alive.[19]

Finally, she risked sending a letter using another name and address.

> Our correspondence began very slowly. The sentences were just "I am fine. Everything is OK." That's it. Nothing else. But finally she found out that I am in America with three daughters and I'm at Harvard, and all that. So she became very happy. After Stalin's death it became easier, but still it was risky to correspond. Each letter was photographed, each letter was studied...[20]

In 1960, in order to see her mother after sixteen years, Marija became an exchange scholar with Hungary and the Union of the Soviet Socialist Republic, where she attended an International Orientalist Congress in Moscow. Their first meeting in Moscow was wrenching because they had to pretend not to know each other, while in the continual presence of spies. Other more satisfying reunions were later arranged in Lithuania through academic channels.

In 1960 after she returned, Marija Gimbutas was awarded the Outstanding New American Award for excellence in scholarship by the World Refugee Committee and Boston Junior Chamber of Commerce. She was also chosen from forty top scholars to be in residence at Stanford University in California as a Fellow of the Center for Advanced Study in the Behavioral Sciences.

Marija devoted the 1961–1962 academic year at Stanford to the preparation of the six-pound tome, *Bronze Age Cultures of Central and Eastern Europe*. Because she was unable to afford a draftsman, her mother paid for hundreds of illustrations that were drawn in Lithuania and sent to California, to complete this enormous work. Marija returned to Harvard to be a lecturer in the Department of Anthropology.

In 1963, when she accepted a position at the University of California at Los Angeles, she left her husband and moved to California with her two youngest daughters. Danutė was already a university student in California. In that same year Marija's book, *The Balts*, appeared in the series called "Ancient Peoples and Places," and a parallel work, *The Slavs*, was sponsored by the American Council of Learned Studies.

According to a colleague, Dr. Jaan Puhvel, the arrival of Dr. Marija Gimbutas at UCLA from Harvard "meant the proximity and participation of the one person who was, even then, revolutionizing the study of East European archaeology, and was laying the groundwork of a new synthesis of "the Indo-European question.'" Inspired by Marija's interdisciplinary approach, Dr. Puhvel and she immediately began to collaborate, "trying to conceptualize a unified field of Indo-European study—one that would bring together . . . archaeology, linguistics, philology, and the study of non-material cultural antiquities."[21] Marija Gimbutas remained at UCLA as a professor of archaeology until her retirement in 1989.

During those exceedingly active years, these two colleagues established the Institute of Archaeology, a program of Indo-European studies, and the Graduate Interdepartmental Program. Dr. Gimbutas served as Chair of European Archaeology, taught Baltic and Slavic studies (including language, mythology, and folklore), Indo-European Studies, and was Curator of Old World Archaeology at the Cultural History Museum at UCLA. She continued to write articles for numerous professional publications and encyclopedias, acted as editor for the *Journal of Indo-European Studies*, and other publication. She also attended yearly international conferences and symposia.

Most of all, Marija Gimbutas was an inspiring teacher who actively encouraged the budding careers of many young archaeologists and linguists. She encouraged her students to develop an interdisciplinary approach in contrast to traditional academia. "Her seminars were always relaxed affairs," recalls archaeologist Karlene Jones-Bley. Students always brought wine and food to share, "but despite the relaxed atmosphere, she always expected work to be accomplished . . . Her memory and encyclopedic knowledge were awe inspiring. You could argue with her opinions, but there was no point in arguing a fact. She was always right. Marija was a woman of very strong opinions, but [this] did not get in the way of giving her students freedom to express their opinions."[22]

Although Marija Gimbutas was primarily known as a world-class Indo-European scholar, her experiences as an excavator, between 1967 and 1980, inspired her to develop new research on the neolithic cultures of southeastern Europe.[23] In 1967–1968, Marija Gimbutas began thirteen years of intensive investigation by becoming project director for excavations of neolithic sites in Yugoslavia and Macedonia, which were sponsored by the Smithsonian Institute with a Humanities Endowment Award. This marked an important turning point in her career.

In 1968, she created another opportunity to visit her mother in Kaunas by becoming an exchange professor with the Union of the Soviet Socialist Republic through the American Academy of Sciences. While there, she accepted an informal invitation to lecture on her work. It was exceedingly rare for presentations to be given by Western scholars during that time.

I spoke about mythology and the Indo-Europeans—not Stalin, Marx or Engels. There were crowds of people sitting on window sills, on the floor, everywhere around me. The room was full with such an excitement . . .[24]

Marija returned home to receive the prestigious *Los Angeles Times's* Woman of the Year Award.

Books by Marija Gimbutas were strictly forbidden in Lithuania during the Soviet period. They were "buried in dark special book depositories of Lithuanian libraries, and it was necessary to get a special permission from a special service in order to have a glimpse at a specific part of a specific text . . . "[25]

Nevertheless, clandestine copies of *Ancient Symbolism* and *The Balts* were secretly passed around. According to Dr. Adomas

Butrimas of Vilnius Art Academy, "*The Balts* remains to this day the best information available . . . and is still used as 'required reading' since we have no other text that presents Baltic prehistory, language and mythology in such a complete and concentrated manner." *The Balts* has been published in English (1963), Italian (1967), German (1991), Portuguese (1991), and Latvian (1994).

During her years of intense travel, lecturing, research, and writing, Marija Gimbutas made an intensive study of thousands of artifacts from neolithic excavations. This material spoke of an ancient aesthetic, entirely different from Bronze-Age burial goods as described in her earlier books.

> I came to a point when I had to understand what was happening in Europe before the arrival of the Indo-Europeans. It was a very gradual process. I did not know then that I would write about neolithic religion or the Goddess. I was only trying to answer this question. During my excavations I became aware that a culture existed that was the opposite of all that was known to be Indo-European. So this led me to coin the new term "Old Europe."[26]

Between 1968 and 1980, Marija Gimbutas directed four other major excavations in southeast Europe: 1968–1969—the Karanovo and Early Bronze Age tell (circa 5000–2000 B.C.) at Sitagroi in Greek Macedonia; 1969–1971—the Starevo and Vina settlement (6300–5000 B.C.) at Anza, Macedonia; 1973–1975—the Sesklo tell at Achilleion, near Farsala, Thessaly, Greece (circa 6500–5600 B.C.); and 1977-1980—the Scaloria cave sanctuary near Manfredonia in southeastern Italy (5600–5300 B.C.). She completely devoted herself to a thorough investigation of the material culture, social structure, and ideology of these earliest agrarian cultures of Europe.

DECIPHERMENT

It became obvious to Marija Gimbutas that every aspect of Old European cultures reflected a sophisticated religions symbolism. Although it is considered to be highly speculative in mainstream archaeology to interpret the ideology of prehistoric societies, it did not satisfy her to measure the typology of vessels nor to date the layers of stratigraphy. She sought to understand the patterns of mythological imagery that could reveal the inner cohesion of this symbolic system.

To adequately investigate Old European culture and symbolism, Marija Gimbutas created an interdisciplinary mode of inquiry which she called "archaeomythology." This process of decipherment utilized the results of her own excavations and an exhaustive synthesis of many hundreds of monographs. It also drew from her an encyclopedic knowledge of folklore, mythology, linguistics, and historical documents—informed by her studies in Lithuania. Her first book to address the significance of neolithic art was *The Gods and Goddesses of Old Europe: 7000–3500 B.C.* (Gimbutas 1974), which was republished in 1982 as *The Goddesses and Gods of Old Europe—Myths and Cult Images.*

A Fulbright Fellowship allowed Marija Gimbutas to return to Lithuania for two months in the spring of 1981 as one of the first Westerners to teach at Vilnius University. She lectured on her recent excavations as well as "Archaeology in the Baltic Area," "Old Europe and the Indo-Europeans," "Baltic Mythology," and other topics.

As she approached the university for her first lecture, hundreds of students stood on either side, showering her with flowers. At the second lecture, thousands of people arrived and most were turned away by the officials.

> There were no ads that I was coming; this was all by word of mouth. The Soviets had not completely exterminated us. It was such a resistance by the younger generation who were yearning for real worth . . . because all they were getting was junk. History did not exist there; it was all distorted.[27]

During her lectures, Baltic prehistory was presented in the context of a broad, European perspective which was shown to be no less developed than Slavic, or any other prehistoric culture. Moreover, ancient Lithuanian heritage was presented as a rich blend of both the patriarchal, sky-oriented Indo-European, and the matristic, earth-oriented Old European layers. The articulation of the differences between these two systems—which is one of Marija Gimbutas's great contributions—provides an essential key for the understanding of the hybridization of European cultural development. Gimbutas's scholarship also influenced the growth of Lithuanian mythological studies and revealed the centrality of female images that have survived in the most ancient ethnographic material.

In response to the overwhelming interest in these lectures, Marija accepted invitations from ten institutions and museums for presentations that were attended by an estimated twenty thousand persons.[28] She also met with many of the archaeologists, ethnographers, and folklorists of Vilnius.

> The most cordial and inspiring contacts were . . . with the artists [who] attended my lectures, invited me to their studios, painted portraits of me, and duplicated my slides of prehistoric art and mythical imagery.[29]

The significance of these presentations for Lithuanians still living under the Soviet system cannot be underestimated.

Very little investigation had been done at that time by European or American scholars on the radical changes that took place in Europe after the appearance of Indo-European influences. In 1979, Marija Gimbutas organized the first interdisciplinary conference on "The Transformation of European and Anatolian Culture, 4500–2500 B.C." held in Dubrovnik, Yugoslavia. This conference, and others that followed, were created to stimulate new research on the radical shift of economic, religious, and social structures that took place between the fifth and third millennia B.C. The second international conference took place in Dublin, Ireland, in 1989. The third—"The Indo-Europeanization of Northern Europe"—was held in Marija's honor in Vilnius, Lithuania, in 1994, the same year as her death.

In 1988, Marija Gimbutas lectured on "The Pre-Christian Religion of Lithuania" at the Vatican in Rome on the occasion of the celebration of six-hundred years of Christianity in Lithuania. She returned to Vilnius in the same year, and lectured on "The Old Mythology of the Balts" for the Union of Lithuanian Artists. The Old European layer of Baltic mythology—which is much deeper than the militaristic, Indo-European layer—expresses the cyclic patterns of nature which are continually renewed. Marija often emphasized, in coded phrases, the importance of drawing strength and inspiration from the wisdom and beauty of the ancient Lithuanian culture, and for cultivating an intellectual preparation necessary for independence.

After years of concentrated work, *The Language of the Goddess* (Gimbutas 1989) was released in time for the international conference in Dublin which she had organized. This beautifully rendered book presents a complex iconography of the spirituality of the Old European Great Goddess, who is all of Nature, as expressed in numerous manifestations. Gimbutas's intention in this book was to "decipher the mythological thought which is the *raison d'être* of this art and basis of its form" (Gimbutas 1989).

REVELATION

According to Marija Gimbutas, the earliest cultures of Europe were peaceful, matristic, primarily egalitarian, and producers of a sophisticated art that reflected an earth-based spirituality, fostering a sacred balance between nature and the human community. The powers of birth-giving, death-wielding, and regeneration were primarily expressed in female forms.

Although Dr. Gimbutas's thesis was not motivated by feminist theory, thousands of people throughout the world have recognized its implications for liberation from systems of domination. The knowledge that humans have lived for thousands of years in balanced societies has made a reorganization of cultural priorities seem possible.

An example of the international excitement generated by Gimbutas's interpretation of Old European symbolism took place in Germany, 1993–1994, during the exhibition, *Sprache der Göttin,* held at the Frauen Museum in Wiesbaden, and inspired by *The Language of the Goddess.* Hundreds of people arrived from all over Europe, and from as far north as Norway, to honor Marija Gimbutas, who was present during the first week of the opening. Later, thousands more traveled from around the world to visit the exhibition—which moved to Bergen, Norway, during the spring of 1995.

In 1991, more than nine hundred people converged at a church in Santa Monica, California, to enthusiastically celebrate the publication of her last book *The Civilization of the Goddess* (Gimbutas 1991). This is her magnum opus—the summary of a great life's work. It is the first book of its kind to examine the way of life, religion, and social structure of Old European cultures (seventh to third millennia B.C.), in contrast to the Indo-European system that entered Europe at the end of the fifth millennium B.C.. Marija Gimbutas accomplished no less than a redefinition of the meaning of civilization:

In my understanding, civilization expresses itself in the creation of what is valuable, not in its destruction; not when half
of humanity is denied the right of expression, when women
are exploited . . . [30]

The importance of Marija Gimbutas for Lithuania was expressed in a special television tribute for her seventieth birthday,
23 January 1991, shortly after independence. On 2 February, a special gathering was held at the Red Auditorium of the Artists'
Mansion in Vilnius which featured an exhibit of large graphic works
by the artist A. Švažas and a presentation of Marija's published
works.

The significance of her vision has been expressed by the
Lithuanian Women's Party, whose program articles state:

Through her work, world-acknowledged Lithuanian scholar
Marija Alseikaitė-Gimbutienė uncovered Old Europe's and
Lithuania's past matristic cultural layer, covered by a patriarchal top-layer of the latest millennia. She showed the importance of returning to this culture, for humanity to strive to
cease waging war and destruction and to reach a harmony in
the relations between men and women. In realizing the full
worth of both gender's self-expression, they can both develop
freely and improve. The Lithuanian Women's Party is a
matristic, non-patriarchal culture's party . . . "[31]

Regardless of her great achievements, Marija Gimbutas was
acutely aware that the potential for knowledge is vast, and the
contributions of a single individual are limited. She possessed a
"humility in the face of the evidence" which caused her to continually revise her own conclusions based upon the most current data.[32] She perceived her work as a beginning, not as an end,
and she knew that many younger scholars would stand on her
shoulders.

Scholarship is not a static thing, it is always changing. The
search for truth continues; we are just the little link in a
chain. You have to look for truth all the time; this is our
purpose. This is the dynamic dance of creativity. Do not be
conservative or imitative. Don't be sheep, repeating what the
others say. I never did that in my life—and I don't want the
younger students to do it. If they like what I accomplished,

that is very good. But take the best of my work and continue with your own work. That's it![33]

Although Marija Gimbutas was frail from years of struggling with cancer, the enormous love and respect she received from thousands of admirers throughout the world—and especially from Lithuania—sustained her until her death in Los Angeles on 2 February 1994. Her ashes were returned to Lithuania and, after ceremonies in both Kaunas and Vilnius, they were buried in the Petrasiunai cemetery in Kaunas beside her mother, Dr. Veronika Janulaitytė-Alseikienė. An estimated three thousand people attended her funeral.

"Now she has returned and belongs to us: A small sand grave on the bank of the Nemunas River, piles of books and the powerful fluttering of Goddess's wings over the ancient land of the Balts . . ."[34]

NOTES

1. Letter to Joan Marler from Ashley Montagu, 28 November 1993.

2. The Secretary General of the League of Nations intervened in 1924 to prevent Danielius Alseikas from being expelled from the Vilnius area by the Polish government.

3. From an interview with Dr. Marija Gimbutas by Dr. Ingė Lukšaitė, published in *Liaudies kultūra* (Lukšaitė 1994). Note that Dr. Jonas Basanavičius, was a medical doctor and folklorist, and was the first person to sign the Lithuanian Declaration of Independence in 1918.

4. This, and all subsequent quotations by Marija Gimbutas that appear in this article are from interviews recorded by Joan Marler between 1987 and 1993.

5. Marija's parents were sophisticated intellectuals who valued folkloric material without being believers. For the servants, who told Marija hundreds of stories, the pagan deities were real.

6. Gimbutas, interview.

7. Gimbutas, interview.

8. Gimbutas, interview.

9. Gimbutas, interview.

10. Gimbutas, interview.

11. Dr. Meilė Lukčienė quoted during the tribute to Marija Gimbutas broadcast on Lithuanian television on the occasion of Dr. Gimbutas's seventieth birthday, 23 January 1991. Translated by Indrė Antanaitis.

12. Gimbutas, interview.

13. Information from a conversation with Jurgis Gimbutas, 23 September 1994.

14. Gimbutas, interview.

15. Forward by Edgar C. Polomé in *Proto-Indo-European: The Archaeology of a Linguistic Problem—Studies in Honor of Marija Gimbutas* (Skomal and Polomé, 1987).

16. Gimbutas, interview.

17. Michael Herity and Georgio Buccellati, quoted from the Memorial Service for Marija Gimbutas, held at the University of California at Los Angeles, 3 March 1994.

18. From "Marija Gimbutas and the Archaeology of the Balts," by Adomas Butrimas in *From the Realm of the Ancestors* (1997).

19. Gimbutas, interview.

20. Gimbutas, interview.

21. Recollection of Dr. Jaan Puhvel at UCLA memorial for Gimbutas, 1994.

22. Recollection of Dr. Karlene Jones-Bley at UCLA memorial for Gimbutas, 1994.

23. "Neolithic" means "new stone age"—which refers to the use of ground stone tools. Neolithic cultures are usually typified by stable agricultural or horticultural communities. Marija Gimbutas roughly dates the Neolithic period in southeast Europe between 6500 and 3500 B.C. In northern Europe, the dates are somewhat later, and they are often defined by the appearance of ceramics.

24. Gimbutas, interview.

25. From "Marija Gimbutas in My life: Some Reminiscences," by Gintautas Česnys, in *From the Realm of the Ancestors* (1997).

26. Gimbutas, interview.

27. Gimbutas, interview.

28. From the final report to the Council for International Exchange of Scholars concerning Dr. Gimbutas's professional activities in Lithuania and Siberia. UCLA, spring semester, 1981.

29. Česnys, 1997.

30. Marija Gimbutas speaking at a public meeting at the Education and Culture Department, Vilnius University, conducted by Prof. Norbertas Velius, June, 1993. Translated by Indrė Antanaitis.

31. From the Lithuanian Women's Party program articles, p. 8. Translated by Indrė Antanaitis.

32. From a conversation with archaeologist Michael Herity, recorded by Joan Marler, 15 March 1992.

33. Gimbutas, interview.

34. Česnys, 1997.

REFERENCES

Butrimas, Adomas
1997. "Marija Gimbutas and the Archaeology of the Balts." In *From the Realm of the Ancestors: An Anthology in Honor of Marija Gimbutas.* Manchester, Conn.: Knowledge, Ideas & Trends, Inc.

Campbell, Joseph
1989. "Foreword." In M. Gimbutas, *The Language of the Goddess.* San Francisco: Harper & Row.

Česnys, Gintautas
1997. "Marija Gimbutas in My Life: Some Reminiscences." In *From the Realm of the Ancestors: An Anthology in Honor of Marija Gimbutas.* Manchester, Conn.: Knowledge, Idea & Trends, Inc.

Gimbutas, Marija
1974. *The Gods and Goddesses of Old Europe.* London: Thames & Hudson.
1982. *The Goddesses and Gods of Old Europe.* Berkeley: University of California.
1989. *The Language of the Goddess.* San Francisco: Harper & Row.
1991. *The Civilization of the Goddess.* San Francisco: Harper.

Lukšaitė, Ingė
1994. "Iš paskutiniųjų profesorės Marijos Gimbutienės susitikimų su Lietuvos žmonemis 1993 met birželio menesi." An interview with

Gimbutas, translated by André Antana it is. *Liaudies kultūra*. (Folk Culture) no. 2.

Skomal, Susan N., and Polomé, Edgar C.
  1987. *Proto-Indo-European: The Archaeology of a Linguistic Problem—Studies in Honor of Marija Gimbutas*. Washington, D.C.: Institute for the Study of Man.

Steinfels, Peter
  1990. "Idyllic Theory Creates Storm." *New York Times*, 13 February.

Notes on Contributors

Viktorija Baršauskienė, Ph.D., Dean of the Faculty of Administration at Kaunas University of Technology, is author of four scholarly texts on business and women's employment.

Dalia Gineitienė is a Lecturer at Kaunas University of Technology.

Renata Guobužaitė is a recent graduate from Kaunas University of Technology. She is currently working on her master's degree in the United States.

Palmira Jucevičienė, Ph.D., Chair of Education and Management at Kaunas University of Technology, is author of five scholarly texts.

Vida Kanopienė, Ph.D., Chair of Sociology at Vilnius University, has conducted research and published articles about women in the labor market.

Suzanne LaFont, Ph.D., editor, was a Visiting Assistant Professor at Kaunas University of Technology during the 1994–1995 academic year. She is an Assistant Professor at Kingsborough Community College, City University of New York. She is the author of *The Emergence of an Afro-Caribbean Legal Tradition* (Austin & Winfield 1996) and several academic articles.

Joan Marler worked closely with Marija Gimbutas since 1987. She edited *The Civilization of the Goddess* (Gimbutas 1991), and *From the Realm of the Ancestors: Essays in Honor of Marija Gimbutas* (1997).

Agnė Pankūnienė recently graduated from Kaunas University of Technology.

Marija Aušrinė Pavilionienė, Ph.D., Director of Women's Study Centré at Vilnius University, is author of several articles on women's studies.

Giedrė Purvaneckienė, Ph.D., was special consultant to the Lithuanian Parliament on women's issues. She is now working at the Women's Information Centre, and is completing research on women and the family.

Giedrė Rymeikytė is a master's student at Kaunas University of Technology.

Dalia Teišerskytė is Chairperson of the Council of the Women's Party in Lithuania.

Dalia Vyšniauskienė, Ph.D., Professor at Kaunas University of Technology, is author of two texts on education and sociology.

Index